EXPRESS REVIEW GUIDES

Writing

New York

Library of Congress Cataloging-in-Publication Data:
Express review guides. Writing.—1st ed.
p. cm.
ISBN: 978-1-57685-627-7
1. English language—Rhetoric—Problems, exercises, etc. 2. Report writing—Problems, exercises, etc. I. LearningExpress (Organization)
PE1417.E98 2007
808'.0427—dc22

2007017307

Printed in the United States of America

9 8 7 6 5 4 3 2 1

First Edition

ISBN: 978-1-57685-627-7

For more information or to place an order, contact LearningExpress at:
55 Broadway
8th Floor
New York, NY 10006

Or visit us at:
www.learnatest.com

Contents

Introduction

This is a book about writing. Yes, I know, you can tell that from the title. So let me get a bit more specific. This is a book about how to craft an essay that's well organized; has a clear point; and is free of grammatical, spelling, and other errors. It covers everything from how to tackle that blank sheet of paper to how to construct a good paragraph to how not to panic if you have only three hours until your essay is due.

There are a couple of major reasons why knowing how to write a logical, interesting, error-free essay is important. One is that you will invariably need to write an essay, and *not* knowing how to write a good one will result in confusion, frustration, dissatisfaction, and many other long, disagreeable nouns. Essay writing will be a much more pleasant experience if you are already familiar with the task at hand and feel comfortable expressing yourself in writing.

Which leads me to the second reason why the ability to write a good essay, as opposed to a bad essay, is an important addition to the repertoire of skills that you've been amassing over the years. The ability to express yourself accurately in writing is almost as basic as the ability to express yourself through speech. Imagine, if every time you spoke, the people around you had no idea what you were trying to say. That would also, no doubt, result in a lot of disagreeable nouns. Whether the vehicle of expression is speech or writing, when you have something important to say—or maybe even something not so important—it is not only satisfying, but also essential that others understand you.

This book will equip you with the basic tools you will need to build an essay that is clear and logical and worthy of your pride. This book also includes the following helpful hints and exercises to help you further develop your writing skills:

- *Fuel for Thought*: critical information and definitions that can help you learn more about a particular topic
- *Inside Track*: tips for reducing your study and practice time—without sacrificing accuracy
- *Caution!*: pitfalls to be on the lookout for
- *Pace Yourself*: extra activities for added practice
- *Practice Lap*: quick practice exercises and activities to let you test your knowledge

The chapters, which include lessons along with examples and practice questions, are meant to be read in order, so the lessons build upon each other as you read. Here's a brief description of each chapter, so that you get an idea of the flow.

CHAPTER 1: PRETEST

Take this test to see where you need to focus before you start the book. Any surprises? This will give you a good idea of your strengths as well as the areas in which you need to improve. Read through each lesson, do the practice questions along the way, and you're bound to strengthen your writing skills.

CHAPTER 2: OUTLINING AND ORGANIZING

This chapter is about how to start an essay, or basically how to go from nothing to something good. It will explain how to gather your ideas and organize them into what will serve as a blueprint for your essay.

CHAPTER 3: ESSAY DEVELOPMENT

What are the parts of an essay? How do you arrange those parts? How can you be confident that people know what your point is? These are the types of questions that will be answered in this chapter.

CHAPTER 4: SENTENCE COMPLETION

You can't write an essay without sentences, and this chapter will explain what makes a sentence complete. It will also delve into sentence completion questions, which you will probably see on at least a test or two. They can be intimidating, but with a few hints, you'll master them in no time.

CHAPTER 5: GRAMMAR

Grammar is the subject we all love to hate, but it is an essential aspect of the ultimate goal. No essay is a good essay without correct grammar. This chapter will explain some common grammatical errors and how to avoid them.

CHAPTER 6: TRICKY WORDS

English is one of the most complicated languages out there. Even if you're fluent, you'll still get tripped up on some tricky words. This chapter attempts to clear up some of the confusion.

CHAPTER 7: PASSIVE VOICE VERSUS ACTIVE VOICE

What are the active and passive voices? When are you supposed to use them? Read this chapter to find out.

CHAPTER 8: REVISING AND EDITING

Revising and editing may be the most important step in the writing process. This chapter will explain how to revise and edit and why this step is so crucial.

CHAPTER 9: WRITING PROMPTS

If you don't know what a writing prompt is, don't worry. This chapter will tell you what they are and what to do with them.

CHAPTER 10: TIMED AND UNTIMED ESSAY WRITING STRATEGIES

It would be nice to have an endless amount of time to write an essay, but we never do. This chapter will take you step by step through the process of getting it done on time, whether you have one month or one hour.

CHAPTER 11: POSTTEST

Now that you've finished the book, how much have you improved? This posttest will give you a chance to see how much you've learned and how far you've come since you took the pretest. Do you still need some improvement? Go back to the relevant chapters and review.

CHAPTER 12: GLOSSARY

This chapter contains an extensive list of important words you may already know, or you may have learned throughout this book. Refer to it as often as you need to.

Ready? Let's get started!

Pretest

This pretest contains 53 questions and is designed to test your knowledge of various topics that are covered in the book. By taking this test and then checking your answers against the answer key that follows, you'll be able to determine what you already know and what you need to learn. For each question you answer incorrectly, be sure to read the explanation that accompanies the correct answer in the answer key. Also, the answer key contains chapter references, so that you know which lesson deals with that question's topic. It should take you no more than two hours to complete the pretest. Good luck!

In the following sentences, circle the word that makes the sentence correct.

1. My glasses, (that/which) are brown, broke yesterday.

2. The pencil has lost (it's/its) eraser.

3. Billy's (parents/parent's) invited me to dinner.

4. I asked my teacher if she and (me/I) could talk after class.

5. It was so cold outside that everybody was wearing (their/his) winter hat.

6. I was tired because I had (run/ran) earlier that morning.

7. We agreed that it made little difference to both her and (I/me).

Identify each of the following sentences as either correct or incorrect.

8. I wanted to turn on the light, but couldn't find it's switch.

9. Gary and me are best friends.

10. My brother has never ate at this restaurant before.

11. Please get me a glass of water; I'm very thirsty.

12. Joe and his mom goes on vacation every summer.

13. His shoelace was untied so he tripped on it.

14. My favorite shirt, which is green, has a new hole in the sleeve.

Rewrite the following sentences to make them correct.

15. I threw the ball to my friend, and she picks it up.

16. The park was crowded with people so I couldn't find an empty bench.

17. I cut myself with a knife cooking dinner.

18. I took all the pictures frames and placed them on the desk that my sister and me share.

19. The lock on the door has been broke for a while, and its frustrating to get into the house.

20. Everyone took off their shoes and jump in the fountain.

For each of the following sentences, choose the correct word to fill in the blank.

21. The art critic found the paintings in the gallery to be so ______________ that he felt like he could have done them himself.

a. uproarious
b. pedestrian
c. sinuous
d. porous
e. peerless

22. The climb up the mountain was so ______________ that the hikers had to take frequent breaks.

a. arduous
b. chauvinist
c. querulous
d. rarefy
e. obviate

23. He was known to be a frequent liar, and his ______________ often got him in trouble.

a. debacle
b. regale
c. mendacity
d. blandishment
e. deposition

24. Although the stock market seemed to be holding steady, there was a ______________ drop this afternoon.

a. quotidian
b. optic
c. surfeit
d. stint
e. precipitous

25. She had been bold in the past and failed, but this time, her ______________ led to success.
a. temerity
b. lapse
c. stanch
d. succor
e. evolution

26. The man in the waiting room was clearly impatient, but his ______________ wouldn't get him in to see the doctor any faster.
a. solitude
b. pensiveness
c. petulance
d. manifesto
e. realism

27. Suzy's ______________ nature made her a perfect candidate for the cheerleading squad.
a. sanguine
b. introspective
c. reverent
d. apathetic
e. restorative

28. The conditions within the volcano are ______________, and scientists think it may erupt any day now.
a. adjacent
b. repute
c. volatile
d. ambitious
e. demented

29. The accused man's testimony was ________________, so the jury thought that he was definitely guilty.

a. cogent
b. bane
c. sundry
d. sentient
e. contradictory

30. Because of his ________________, the dog was able to break through the fence.

a. selectiveness
b. vigor
c. facetiousness
d. pensiveness
e. indolence

31. Even though she apologized for her mistake, the politician was still ________________ by the legislature.

a. undeceived
b. engendered
c. circulated
d. censured
e. congregated

32. The scientific journal was so ________________ that not even the scientist could understand what it said.

a. deranged
b. adorable
c. pertinent
d. sincere
e. recondite

33. The pizza dough wasn't as ______________ as it should have been, so I added some water to make it easier to work with.

a. malleable
b. coherent
c. liberal
d. tranquil
e. erratic

34. People stuffing their faces in eating contests is much too ______________ to watch.

a. pristine
b. flamboyant
c. devious
d. fulsome
e. obsolete

35. When I was out in the ocean, the waves were ______________ so much that I still felt as if I were moving, even when I was back on the beach.

a. undulating
b. placid
c. intriguing
d. necrotic
e. conceding

36. Even the citizens of the town, who usually disagreed with the court's decisions, found its ruling to be ______________.

a. durable
b. pliable
c. frenetic
d. insipid
e. judicious

Identify the topic and focus of the following topic sentences. Circle the topic and put a box around the focus.

37. There are many precautions you should take when working in a science lab.

38. It is not difficult to plant a garden if you follow some simple steps.

39. Softball is a fun sport to play for many reasons.

40. There are many reasons why running inside the house can be dangerous.

41. By following some simple steps, you can easily make a turkey sandwich.

Write a topic sentence using each topic and focus listed.

42. Topic = drinking water
Focus = ways it's beneficial to your health

43. Topic = playing checkers
Focus = simple rules for playing

44. Topic = fish are good pets
Focus = reasons fish are good pets

45. Topic = photography is a fun hobby
Focus = reasons it's fun

46. Topic = saving electricity
Focus = reasons it's important to save electricity

Choose the correct answer to the following multiple-choice questions.

47. An inductive paragraph is
- **a.** a paragraph that is well written.
- **b.** a paragraph that begins with the topic sentence.
- **c.** a paragraph that ends with the topic sentence.
- **d.** a paragraph at the end of an essay.

48. When is a good time to start a new paragraph?
- **a.** the top of a new page
- **b.** after each topic sentence
- **c.** whenever you want
- **d.** when discussing a new idea

Read the following paragraph and then answer the questions that follow.

There are many reasons why a person may get excited about a possible snowstorm, but there are also many reasons why a person may dread one. A person may get excited if he or she were a student, because if it snows enough to cancel school, the student would have the day off. On the other hand, a person who has to drive in the snow would not look forward to slipping and sliding all over the road. Some people may enjoy the prospect of going out and playing in the snow, maybe sledding down a hill. I went sledding once, and it was a blast. Others, however, may not enjoy the prospect of having to shovel the snow off their front walks.

49. What is the topic sentence of the paragraph?

50. What kind of paragraph is this?
- **a.** inductive
- **b.** deductive

51. Which sentence in the paragraph is out of place and should be omitted?

Write an essay for each of the following writing prompts.

52. We all have people in our lives whom we admire. Think about a person in your life whom you admire. Explain why you admire that person.

53. You have a friend who is thinking of running for class president. Do you think your friend should run? Write to your friend to persuade him or her of your opinion regarding whether or not he or she should run for class president.

ANSWERS

1. which
The phrase set off by the commas is a nonrestrictive clause, so *which* is the correct word to use in this instance. (For more information on this concept, see Chapter 5.)

2. its
The eraser belongs to the pencil; therefore, *it* should be possessive and without an apostrophe. (For more information on this concept, see Chapter 5.)

3. parents
This sentence refers to both of Billy's parents, a noun that is plural, not possessive, and should not have an apostrophe. (For more information on this concept, see Chapter 5.)

4. I
When testing the sentence with the pronouns individually, you find that you would say *I could talk*, and not *Me could talk*. (For more information on this concept, see Chapter 5.)

5. his
Everybody refers to one group of people, so it should be paired with a singular pronoun. (For more information on this concept, see Chapter 5.)

6. run
Run is an irregular verb, and when used in the past participle form, it becomes *had run*. (For more information on this concept, see Chapter 5.)

7. me

Again, for this sentence, just test it out using the pronouns individually. It would be incorrect to say *It made little difference to I*, so *me* is correct. (For more information on this concept, see Chapter 5.)

8. incorrect

The switch belongs to the light, so *it's* should be the possessive form, which would be *its*. The correct sentence should read, *I wanted to turn on the light, but couldn't find its switch*. (For more information on this concept, see Chapter 5.)

9. incorrect

The sentence should read *Gary and* I *are best friends*. You wouldn't say that *Me am a best friend*. (For more information on this concept, see Chapter 5.)

10. incorrect

Eat is an irregular verb whose past participle form is *has eaten*. (For more information on this concept, see Chapter 5.)

11. correct

These are two independent clauses that are correctly separated by a semicolon. (For more information on this concept, see Chapter 5.)

12. incorrect

Joe and his mom are two people, so this phrase needs to be paired with a plural form of the verb, which is *go*. The sentence should read, *Joe and his mom go on vacation every summer*. (For more information on this concept, see Chapter 5.)

13. incorrect

These are two independent clauses that need to be separated by either a semicolon or a period. (For more information on this concept, see Chapter 5.)

14. correct

Which is green is a nonrestrictive clause and is correctly set apart from the rest of the sentence using commas. (For more information on this concept, see Chapter 5.)

15. I threw the ball to my friend, and she picked it up.

The two verbs in the sentence need to agree. If I threw the ball in past tense, then she would need to pick it up in past tense. (For more information on this concept, see Chapter 5.)

16. The park was crowded with people, so I couldn't find an empty bench. *The park was crowded with people* is an introductory clause and needs to be set apart from the rest of the sentence by a comma. (For more information on this concept, see Chapter 5.)

17. While cooking dinner, I cut myself with a knife.
In the incorrect version of this sentence, a misplaced modifier makes it seem as if the knife were cooking dinner. Rearranging the sentence clears up the confusion. (For more information on this concept, see Chapter 5.)

18. I took all the pictures' frames and placed them on the desk that my sister and I share.
If there are multiple pictures, then the word *picture* becomes plural and possessive, which means it needs an *s* and then an apostrophe. Also, it is correct to say *I share* something, not *me share* something, so *my sister and I* is correct. (For more information on this concept, see Chapter 5.)

19. The lock on the door has been broken for a while, and it's frustrating to get into the house.
In this sentence, the verb *broke* is being used with the helping verb *has*, which means it needs to be in past participle form. The past participle form of *broke* is *broken*. Also, *its* here is being used as a contraction for *it is* and, therefore, needs an apostrophe. (For more information on this concept, see Chapter 5.)

20. Everyone took off her shoes and jumped in the fountain.
Everyone is singular, so *her* should be used instead of the plural *their*. Also, the verb tenses in the sentence need to agree, so *jump* should be *jumped*. (For more information on this concept, see Chapter 5.)

21. **b.** This is a cause-and-effect sentence completion question. Ask yourself, what could the paintings have been like that they caused the art critic to think he could have done them himself? *Pedestrian* means ordinary or uninspired. (For more information on this concept, see Chapter 4.)

22. **a.** This is another cause-and-effect sentence completion question. What could the climb have been like that it would have caused the hikers to take frequent breaks? *Arduous* means difficult or strenuous. (For more information on this concept, see Chapter 4.)

23. **c.** This is a restatement sentence completion question. The word you are looking for is defined in the sentence. We know that he is a frequent liar, and *mendacity* means dishonesty. (For more information on this concept, see Chapter 4.)

24. **e.** This is a contrast sentence completion question. The answer will be the opposite of what is already defined in the sentence. *Precipitous* means to drop sharply, which is contrary to holding steady. (For more information on this concept, see Chapter 4.)

25. **a.** This is a restatement sentence completion question. We know that she had been bold and failed and that this time the same characteristic led to her success. So we are looking for a word that means to be bold. *Temerity* means boldness or nerve. (For more information on this concept, see Chapter 4.)

26. **c.** This is another restatement sentence completion question. We know the man is impatient, so we are looking for a word that has the same meaning. *Petulance* means irritability or impatience. (For more information on this concept, see Chapter 4.)

27. **a.** This is a cause-and-effect sentence completion question. What characteristic did Suzy have that caused her to be a perfect candidate for the cheerleading squad? *Sanguine* means cheerful or upbeat. (For more information on this concept, see Chapter 4.)

28. **c.** This is a cause-and-effect sentence completion question. What condition does the volcano have that makes scientists think it may erupt? *Volatile* means unstable or explosive. (For more information on this concept, see Chapter 4.)

29. **e.** This is a cause-and-effect sentence completion question. What about the man's testimony would cause the jury to think he was guilty? *Contradictory* means paradoxical or conflicting. (For more information on this concept, see Chapter 4.)

30. **b.** This is a cause-and-effect sentence completion question. What characteristic did the dog have that made it able to break through the fence? *Vigor* means strength. (For more information on this concept, see Chapter 4.)

31. **d.** This is a contrast sentence completion question. The answer should be in contrast to the politician apologizing. *Censured* means criticized or reprimanded. (For more information on this concept, see Chapter 4.)

32. **e.** This is a cause-and-effect sentence completion question. What characteristic could the journal have had that would have caused the scientists not to understand it? *Recondite* means obscure. (For more information on this concept, see Chapter 4.)

33. **a.** This is a restatement sentence completion question. The answer is already defined for you in the sentence. Adding the water made the dough easier to work with. So the characteristic the pizza dough lacked was one that means easy to work with. *Malleable* means flexible or compliant. (For more information on this concept, see Chapter 4.)

34. **d.** This is a cause-and-effect sentence completion question. What characteristic of eating contests would cause someone not to watch them? *Fulsome* means excessive. (For more information on this concept, see Chapter 4.)

35. **a.** This is a cause-and-effect sentence completion question. What characteristic did the waves have that they made me feel as if like I were moving even when I left the water? *Undulating* means rising and falling. (For more information on this concept, see Chapter 4.)

36. **e.** This is a comparison sentence completion question. The citizens usually disagreed, but this time, they didn't. The fact that this time they agreed is directly related to the meaning of the correct word. *Judicious* means fair. (For more information on this concept, see Chapter 4.)

37. FOCUS TOPIC

There are many [precautions] you should take when (working in a science lab).

Working in a science lab is the topic, and the precautions you should take while working in the lab is the focus. (For more information on this concept, see Chapter 3.)

38. TOPIC FOCUS

It is not difficult to (plant a garden) if you follow some [simple steps].

Planting a garden is the topic, and the steps involved in planting the garden is the focus. (For more information on this concept, see Chapter 3.)

39. TOPIC FOCUS FOCUS

(Softball) is a [fun] sport to play for many [reasons].

Softball is the topic, and the reasons why it's a fun sport is the focus. (For more information on this concept, see Chapter 3.)

40. FOCUS TOPIC FOCUS
There are many [reasons] why (running inside the house) can be [dangerous].
Running inside the house is the topic, and reasons why running inside the house can be dangerous is the focus. (For more information on this concept, see Chapter 3.)

41. FOCUS TOPIC
By following some [simple steps], you can easily (make a turkey sandwich).
Making a turkey sandwich is the topic, and the steps involved in making a turkey sandwich is the focus. (For more information on this concept, see Chapter 3.)

42. There are many ways in which drinking water can be beneficial to your health.
This is just an example of what your sentence may look like. Just make sure you've included the topic and the focus in the sentence. (For more information on this concept, see Chapter 3.)

43. Checkers is a game that can be played by following some simple rules.
You need to include the topic, which is checkers, and the focus, which is the rules for playing. (For more information on this concept, see Chapter 3.)

44. Fish make good pets for a variety of reasons.
If you've included the fact that fish make good pets and stated that there are reasons they make good pets, then you've got a topic sentence. (For more information on this concept, see Chapter 3.)

45. There are many reasons why photography is a fun hobby.
Make sure your sentence includes the fact that photography is fun and that there are reasons it is fun. (For more information on this concept, see Chapter 3.)

46. Saving electricity is important for a number of reasons.
This is an example of how you could make the topic and focus into a topic sentence. (For more information on this concept, see Chapter 3.)

47. **c.** Inductive paragraphs end with the topic sentence, and deductive paragraphs begin with the topic sentence. (For more information on this concept, see Chapter 3.)

48. **d.** You should start a new paragraph each time you begin discussing a new idea in your essay. (For more information on this concept, see Chapter 3.)

49. "There are many reasons why a person may get excited about a possible snowstorm, but there are also many reasons why a person may dread one." This is the topic sentence, because it states the topic of the paragraph and the focus of that topic. The topic is a possible snowstorm, and the focus is reasons why someone may either look forward to or dread the thought of a snowstorm. (For more information on this concept, see Chapter 3.)

50. **b.** It is a deductive paragraph, because it begins with the topic sentence. (For more information on this concept, see Chapter 3.)

51. "I went sledding once, and it was a blast."
Although this sentence may introduce an interesting tidbit of information, it is not directly related to the topic of the paragraph. It interrupts the flow of the writing by taking the reader off topic. (For more information on this concept, see Chapter 3.)

52. *We all know people who, although we may not see them every day, we look up to and admire. Sometimes we even admire sports figures, politicians, or actors, but whomever we admire, it's always someone who we strive to be like in our own way. My aunt Maggie is one of those people to me. Aunt Maggie lives a few towns over, and I see her about once a month on the weekends. The fact that she is good at her job, volunteers in the community, and is an excellent cook are all reasons why I admire my aunt Maggie.*

It's easy to admire someone who is good at her job, and Aunt Maggie is the best. She teaches preschool and works with young kids, and they love her. She's always singing them songs and reading them books. They have a little kitchen at the preschool, so she even has the kids help her make cookies. Being a preschool teacher allows for a lot of creativity, which is one of Aunt Maggie's strong suits. She helps the kids learn basic skills through all sorts of art projects, like finger painting and building with clay.

Aunt Maggie not only helps her students learn through art projects, but helps her community, too, which is another reason I admire her. Aunt Maggie volunteers every other weekend at the animal shel-

ter in her town. She loves animals and is happy to help them in any way she can. At the shelter, she plays with the cats and dogs and assists the workers there by cleaning out the animal cages, so the animals can enjoy a clean environment. Aunt Maggie also helps the animals get adopted into loving homes by taking them to the front of a local grocery store, so potential pet owners can get to know the cats and dogs.

Aunt Maggie has a cat of her own, whom I see when I go over to her house to admire her cooking abilities. She always makes it look so easy. Aunt Maggie learned to cook from her mom, my grandma, and makes the best macaroni and cheese in the world. When I come over, she shows me how to make it, and while it's baking, we make cupcakes to eat for dessert. I admire her cooking skills so much that I hope one day I'll be able to make macaroni and cheese that tastes just like Aunt Maggie's.

Whether it's macaroni and cheese, cupcakes, or any other dish she may cook up, Aunt Maggie's food is the tastiest around. But it's not just her cooking abilities that are admirable; she is a kind person who gives back to her community by helping out at the local animal shelter. I'm not the only one who admires and looks up to Aunt Maggie. All you have to do is spend a few minutes in her preschool class and you'll see it on all those kids' faces. They look up to Aunt Maggie, too.

This essay is just an example of what your answer to the writing prompt may be like. *The fact that she is good at her job, volunteers in the community, and is an excellent cook are all reasons why I admire my aunt Maggie* is the essay's thesis statement and appears as the last sentence of the introduction. Then, all three body paragraphs support the thesis by presenting the reader with examples of how Aunt Maggie is good at her job, what she does to volunteer, and what makes her a good cook. There are no grammatical, spelling, or usage errors in the essay, and it has a good flow from start to finish. The conclusion does a good job of restating the thesis and reminding the reader of what was discussed in the rest of the essay. (For more information on this concept, see Chapter 10 specifically, but *all* the chapters apply!)

53. *The decision to run for class president is a big one, so I'm glad that you are gathering your friends' opinions before you decide either way. You should think about the issues related to running for and being class president before you take the step to put your name on the ballot. How will it affect your time at school? What kind of experience will it be? Would you be able to make a difference in the lives of your fellow students? Well, since you've asked me, I've given it some thought. I think that you should run for class president, because if you win, you'll be able to make changes that would improve the school, the job will give you excellent leadership experience, and you may even receive special treatment from teachers and other students.*

If you were class president, you may have the ability to make changes to the school that you feel would be beneficial to the students. One of the advantages of being class president is the power to influence decisions that are typically made by adults. Often, issues arise at school, whether they be related to the food in the cafeteria or to the kinds of classes that are offered, and the class president gets to speak for the student body on those issues by voicing his or her opinion. Wouldn't it be great if you were able to help make decisions about what classes are offered or what kinds of dances we have?

Making decisions is part of being a leader, and being class president would give you some invaluable leadership experience. By being the leader of the class council, you'll learn skills, such as public speaking, that will be helpful to have later in life. You'll probably have to stand up and speak in front of the class council, if not the entire school, at some point, and that experience will help you become more comfortable speaking in front of large groups of people. The public speaking skills, as well as decision-making and writing skills, that you learn as class president will all be useful later in life when you enter the workforce.

While the leadership experience will be valuable later, the special treatment you may receive from teachers, students, and administrators would be fun right now. As class president, you may have to miss classes to attend various meetings, and your teachers won't get angry because you hold such an important position in school-wide politics. Other students, too, may treat you differently. The title of class president holds with it a certain amount of respect among the student body, so you could even find that you're suddenly more popular with other students than you were before.

Whether it's because of the special treatment, the leadership experience, or the opportunity to make changes to the school, choosing to run for class president is a wise decision. Those all seem like good reasons to run, and I also happen to think that you'd be good at it. It would be fun, and maybe you'd make some new friends in the process. So put your name on that ballot and start the campaign! You could be our next class president!

Again, this essay is just an example. It has a clear thesis statement, which is the last sentence of the introduction; has good flow; and lacks any grammatical, spelling, or usage errors. Each paragraph has a topic sentence that connects not only with the paragraph to follow, but also with the previous paragraph as well as the thesis statement. The conclusion is clear and reiterates the argument of the essay, while leaving the reader excited about the prospect of running for class president. (For more information on this concept, see Chapter 10 specifically, but *all* the chapters apply!)

Outlining and Organizing

The first step in writing any kind of essay is to organize your thoughts and ideas. It's kind of like baking a cake. Without a recipe to tell you what ingredients to use and the order in which to use those ingredients, you may end up with something that resembles a cake, but it probably won't taste very good. The same thing is true of essay writing. Unless you know what the parts of your essay are going to be and in what order you're going to write those parts, you will probably end up with a very disjointed, unclear piece of writing. So, here's some help with organizing your ideas, so that your cake is as tasty as possible!

PREWRITING

Often, the most difficult part of writing is getting started. Sitting and staring at a blank piece of paper or a blank word-processing document can be a lot of pressure. To relieve some of that pressure, try jotting down anything related to your topic that comes to mind. Don't worry about how you phrase it or if it's really what you want to say. All of that will come together later. For now, just write anything. You'll find that, as you write, new ideas and thoughts will come to you. Write those down, too. This is often called a free-write, because it involves writing completely free of any expectations.

PACE YOURSELF

Keep a journal. It's a good way to practice writing your thoughts without editing yourself. Plus, you never know when you may be asked to write about yourself. A journal provides excellent material for a self-reflective essay.

So now you have a bunch of jumbled ideas that somehow relate to your intended topic. Now what? You need to organize all of those great ideas into an order that will form the basis for your eventual essay. You need to sort out your main ideas from your supporting ideas. Maybe you've thought of some examples or anecdotes that you want to include. You need to take all of these components and organize them from a jumble into a web. A web is just one way to organize visually all the components of your essay so that you can start to get a better sense of which thoughts are main ideas and which thoughts are going to play supporting roles.

INSIDE TRACK

Bounce your ideas off someone else. Brainstorming doesn't have to be a solo activity.

WEBBING AND CHARTING

Are you wondering why you should take the time to make a web or a chart? Well, here's why it's helpful. Both webs and charts serve as visual representations of how your ideas relate to one another. Ideas are pretty intangible things. You can't see them or touch them, which makes it difficult to get them organized. Imagine trying to organize your sock drawer without being able to see your socks. Organizing is much easier when you can see everything laid out in front of you. That's what webs and charts do. They allow you to see your ideas and to see how they will support one another in your essay.

Making a Web

Here's how to make a web. Sift through your mess of ideas and find the central idea of your essay. Start by writing that central idea in the middle of a piece of paper.

Qualities a friend
should have

Draw a circle around it, or a rectangle, or even a hexagon. The shape doesn't matter.

Qualities a friend
should have

Then, all around your central idea, write your support for that idea and connect each support to the central idea with a line.

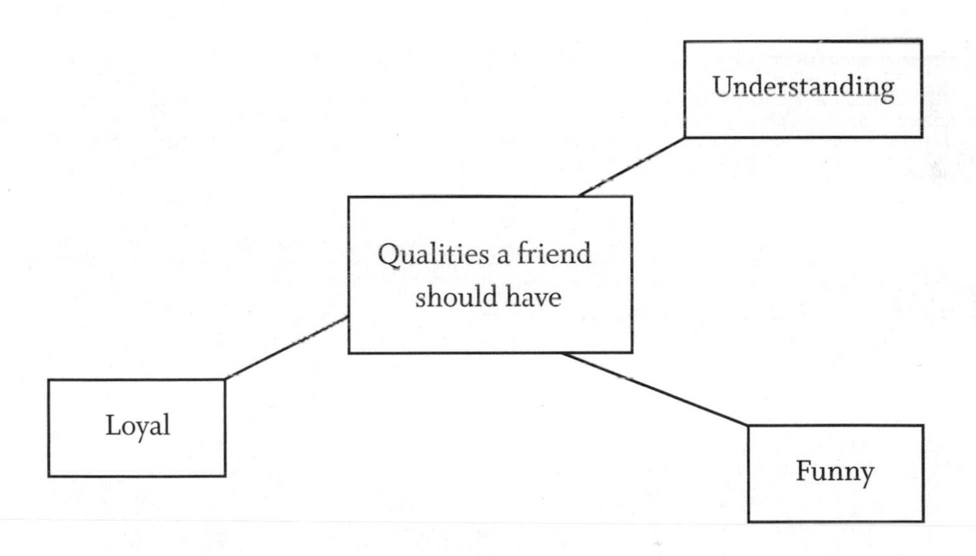

At this point, your web should start to look very weblike. In the previous example, you can see that *Loyal*, *Understanding*, and *Funny* are all examples of *Qualities a friend should have*. Finally, connect some examples or, in this case, reasons to your supporting ideas. Here's what your completed web may look like.

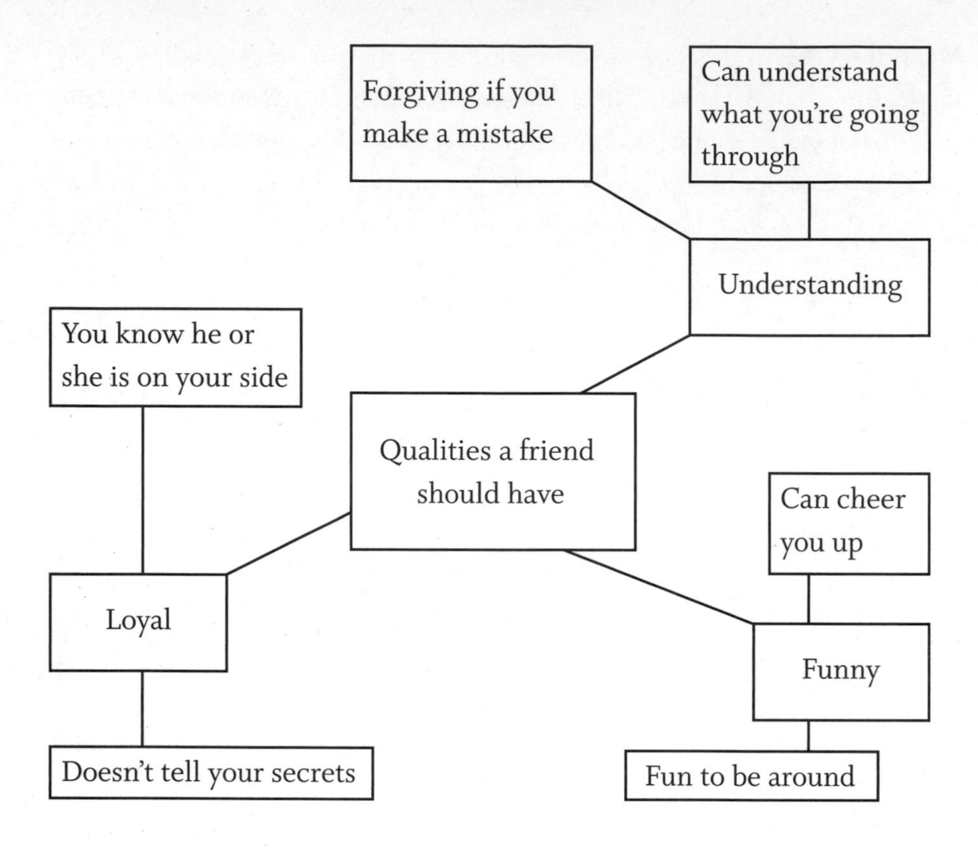

Notice that each quality that a friend should have is linked to two reasons why that's a good quality in a friend. You may have more than two for each. That's fine. The idea is to organize what you have so that you can see how all the information holds itself together.

CAUTION!

Don't get caught up in what your web looks like. No one but you will see it.

Like free-writing, when you're making a web, you don't need to worry about how you phrase your ideas or even which ones you will use. Maybe you've thought of a lot of examples for one of your supporting ideas, but you think some of them may be better than others. That's okay. Just leave them in the web for now. You'll go through them later to weed out all the weak links.

PRACTICE LAP

1. Which of these ideas would go in the middle of a web?
  a. create a menu
  b. buy decorations
  c. how to plan a party
  d. make a guest list

2. Which of the following ideas could NOT be considered a supporting idea for the topic *Advantages of Time Travel*?
  a. can go back and change events in history
  b. may not be able to get home
  c. can see the future
  d. would be a breakthrough in science

3. Use the ideas in this list to fill in the blank web.
Ride bike
Get exercise
Read a book
Learn to swim
Cool off in the water
Fun things to do in the summer
Bike to a friend's house
Go to the pool
Get to read something for pleasure
Stay inside where it's cool

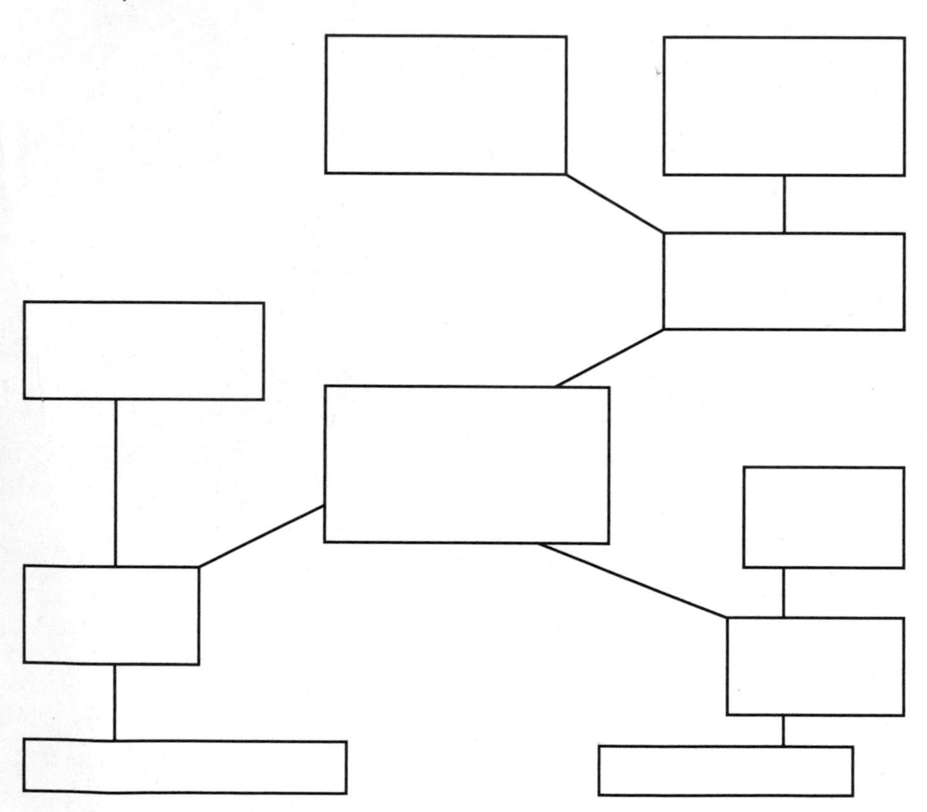

Check your answers on page 31.

Making a Flow Chart

Another tool for organizing your ideas visually is a flow chart, which is sort of like a family tree. Instead of putting your central idea in the middle of the page and branching out from there, in a flow chart, you write your central idea at the top of the page and connect your support and examples in a downward "flow" from there. A flow chart may look like this.

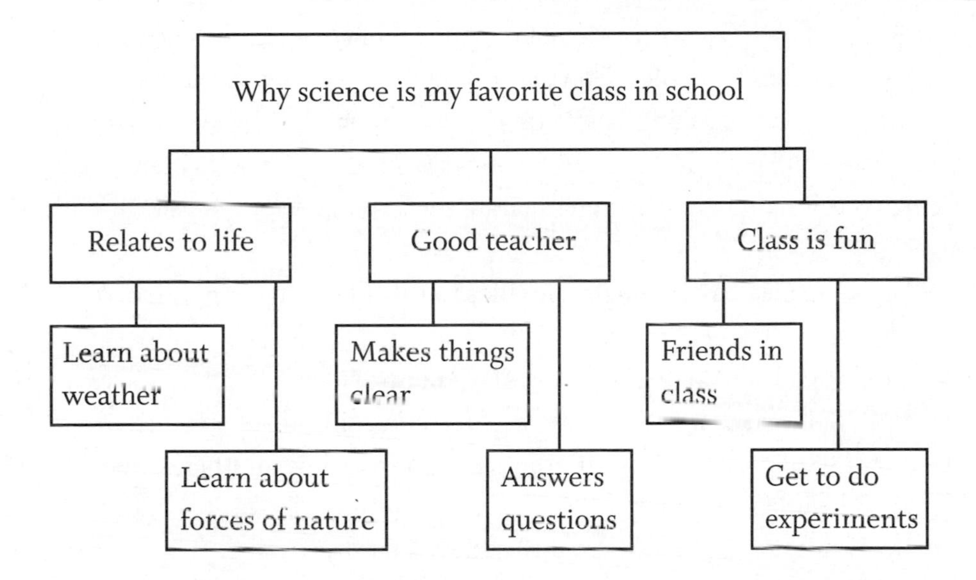

Why science is my favorite class in school is the central idea of the essay, and *Relates to life*, *Good teacher*, and *Class is fun* are all reasons why it is my favorite class. On the third level of the chart, you see two examples for each reason.

Whether you use a web or a flow chart, the key is to organize. Maybe you're a list maker, so just making a list of all your supporting ideas and examples works better for you. Go ahead. Do that. No one is going to see any of this prewriting. It's just for you. Do whatever you can to get your ideas down on paper so that you can see your central idea, support, and examples in an organized way. The goal is to know what the components of your essay will be and in what order you will use them.

EDITING YOUR IDEAS

Okay, so now you've brainstormed ideas and organized all the jumbled mess that came out of your brain into some sort of web or flow chart. Here is where the editing comes in. While there's no doubt you've come up with some fabulous ideas for your essay, you've probably also thought of some clunkers. We need to weed out the clunkers. The easiest way to do this is to go back over your web or flow chart with a highlighter and highlight all the best ideas, best support, and best examples. Don't have a highlighter? Just circle them.

Now you may be asking, "How do I know which ideas are fabulous and which are clunkers?" Here are some questions to ask yourself when you're doing your weeding, to help you separate the two.

- Does the idea have enough examples to fill at least a paragraph of writing?
- Does the idea truly support the essay's central idea?
- Will I get off track when I start writing about this idea?
- Are my supporting ideas different enough from one another, while still all supporting my thesis?
- Do I have enough to say about this idea?

OUTLINING

Before You Outline

You've gone back over your web or chart and highlighted or circled all of your wonderful ideas. So now you know which ideas you're going to use in your essay. That's really all you need to make an outline. An outline is just the next step in organizing your essay.

General Format

Now that we're getting to be master organizers, it's time for the final step in the organizational process: the outline. Don't be afraid of the outline. It's really quite easy. Here is the general format.

I.

    A.

    B.

        1.

        2.

            a.

            b.

II.

    A.

    B.

        1.

        2.

            a.

            b.

Plugging in Your Ideas

To make your outline, all you need to do is plug in your ideas. Your more general supporting ideas or themes go next to the Roman numerals, and then each level gets more specific. Following is an example. As you can see, not all As are followed by a secondary level, and the same holds true with Bs. Some essays will be more involved and need more detailed outlines. Some will be fairly straightforward and not require as many levels of information.

FUEL FOR THOUGHT

Roman numerals

I	= 1	VI	= 6
II	= 2	VII	= 7
III	= 3	VIII	= 8
IV	= 4	IX	= 9
V	= 5	X	= 10

Reasons the new town park is a good idea

I. Safe place for kids to play
  A. No cars
  B. Fence around the perimeter
II. Will preserve some open space
  A. Good for the environment
    1. No car fumes
    2. Homes for animals
  B. The land won't be developed in the future
III. Opportunities for sports
  A. New baseball diamond
  B. There will be grassy open space
    1. Can play Frisbee
    2. Can run races on the grass

Just think, general to specific. The topic of the previous outline is *Reasons the new town park is a good idea*. The ideas next to the Roman numerals are the reasons. In this case, there are three: It will be a safe place for kids to play, it will preserve some open space, and it will provide opportunities for sports. As the outline gets more specific, we can see *how* it will be safe for kids and *why* preserving the open space is good and *what* kinds of sports will be played there. The outline lets us see how everything fits together in support of the topic.

There is one rule to remember when creating an outline. If you have a I, you have to have a II, and if you have an A, you have to have a B, and if you have a 1, you have to have a . . . well, you get the idea.

PACE YOURSELF

Find a newspaper article and turn it into an outline.

When Your Outline Is Complete

When you've finished your outline, look it over and make sure that your major points are addressed and that each point has sufficient support. Think of your supporting ideas as beams holding up the bridge that is your main idea. Without the support, your bridge will crumble.

PRACTICE LAP

4. Which of the following outlines is correctly formatted?

I.	A.	I.
B.	1.	A.
A.	2.	B.
a.	B.	II.
b.		

5. Put the following list in order from general to specific (1 = most general, 5 = most specific).

My favorite mystery writer is Agatha Christie.
Reading is an activity.
Sometimes I read mysteries.
My favorite Agatha Christie novel is *Death on the Nile*.
I like to read.

6. Circle the line of the outline that doesn't make sense.

Time When I Felt Lucky

I. What happened
  A. I lost my watch
  B. Someone returned it to me
II. How I felt
  A. Relieved to have my watch back
  B. The clasp on the watch was broken
  C. Thankful toward the person who returned it

7. Which of the following is NOT true?
   a. An outline is a way of organizing your ideas.
   b. Outlines start with more general ideas and get more specific with each level of information.
   c. Outlines are only necessary for certain essay topics.
   d. If an outline has an A, it must also have a B.
   e. It's helpful to weed out weak ideas before starting your outline.

8. Format the following list of ideas for the essay topic *Places I may want to go on vacation* into an outline.
   The beach
   Hiking
   The mountains
   Skiing
   Swimming
   Building sand castles

9. Which of the following ideas seems out of place?
   Healthier food in the cafeteria
   More time for exercise at school
   Replace soda machines with water machines
   More pizza parties
   Increase number of health education classes

Check your answers on page 32.

LET'S RECAP

Sometimes it may seem like a hassle to have to do all this work before you even start writing your essay. Just remember that this preparation will make the essay easier for you to write, and you'll end up with a clearer, more organized final product. It may even save you time in the long run. Starting can be the hardest part, so just dive right in by doing some free-writing, without stopping to edit yourself. Then, once the juices are flowing, begin organizing your thoughts into a web or chart. Next, make an outline. After each step in the process, go back over what you've written and weed out the weak ideas and examples. By the time you finish your outline, you'll have a complete plan for an essay that's full of all your best ideas. That's the goal.

Writing can definitely be overwhelming sometimes, but by breaking it down into smaller pieces, it's easier to tackle the task. So just think of these little tasks as building blocks. Complete one at a time, and before you know it, you'll have a clear, strong, well-written, interesting essay. Just remember the basic rule of organizing your thoughts, which is to start generally and get more specific.

ANSWERS

1. c. Of the four answer choices, *How to plan a party* is the most general. The other three answer choices would all be steps in the planning process. They wouldn't go in the middle of the web, but rather would be connected to the middle.
2. b. *May not be able to get home* is the only answer choice that could not be considered an advantage to time travel.
3. 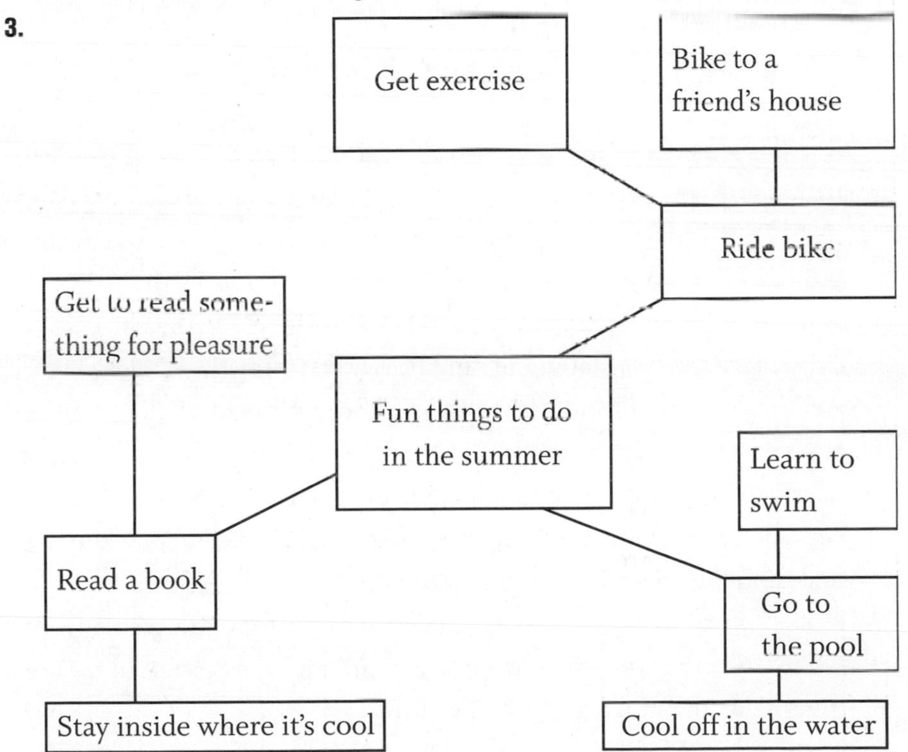

Reading over the phrases that are being used to fill in the web, you can tell that they are all related in some way to the topic *Fun things to do in the summer*. Therefore, you know that should be the center of your web. Of the remaining phrases, *Ride bike*, *Read a book*, and *Go to the pool* are the next most general ideas. All of these activities are fun to do in the summer, so they go on the next branches of the web. Now you know that the remaining phrases will go on the outermost branches of the web. The only thing left to determine is which phrases go with which activity. Staying inside and reading for pleasure could both be related to reading a book. Getting exercise and pedaling to a friend's house are both related to riding a bike. And cooling off in the water and learning to swim are both related to going to the pool.

4. The third outline is correctly formatted because the A and B are in the correct order and indented correctly from the Roman numerals. The first outline is incorrect because B comes before A, and the second outline is incorrect because B should be indented under the A.

5. 4 My favorite mystery writer is Agatha Christie.
1 Reading is an activity.
3 Sometimes I read mysteries.
5 My favorite Agatha Christie novel is *Death on the Nile*.
2 I like to read.
Reading is an activity is the most general statement. *I like to read* gets a little more specific by stating the writer's particular preference. *Sometimes I read mysteries* is even more specific, because it describes the kinds of books the writer sometimes reads. Of the mysteries that the writer sometimes reads, stating that his or her favorite is Agatha Christie is an even more specific statement, and finally, defining the writer's favorite Agatha Christie novel is the most specific statement of all.

6. **b.** The line *The clasp on the watch was broken* is out of place because it has nothing to do with the subject next to the Roman numeral that precedes it. The fact that the clasp was broken is unrelated to how the writer feels about having the watch returned.

7. **c.** It is not true that outlines are necessary only for certain essay topics. No matter what you are writing about, an outline is essential for creating a clear and concise piece of writing.

8. I. The beach

   A. Swimming

   B. Building sand castles

II. The mountains

   A. Skiing

   B. Hiking

The beach and *The mountains* are two places to go on a vacation, so those are going to be the Roman numerals of the outline. As for the four other items, they need to be categorized under *The beach* and *The mountains*. Skiing and hiking are both activities that would be performed in the mountains, so they belong under *The mountains*. Swimming and building sand castles are both activities that would be performed at the beach, so they are listed under *The beach*.

9. *More pizza parties*

The phrase seems out of place, because the four other phrases all relate in some way to being healthier. Having more pizza parties doesn't seem like a way to be healthier.

Essay Development

So you have an outline. Now what? What should you do with it? Well, you should use it as a map. I know, you're thinking, "But it's not a map. It's an outline!" Think about it this way. When you need to go from Point A to Point B and you don't know the route, you use a map. The map tells you what roads to take so that you don't get lost. It guides you. Well, that's exactly what an outline does. It helps you get from your introduction to your conclusion without getting lost along the way.

Keep your map handy while we do a little essay dissection. Before you write your essay, you should probably know what the parts of an essay are.

PARTS OF AN ESSAY

Introduction

In your introduction, you say what you're going to say.

Your **introduction** is the first chance you have to spark your reader's interest and to explain to him or her what you will be discussing in your essay. It's sort of like a movie preview. The object of a movie preview is to introduce you to the movie in an interesting way, so that when you see the preview, you think to yourself, "That movie looks good. I want to watch that." A good preview gives you just enough of a glimpse of who the characters are and what the basic plot is that it leaves you wanting more. An introduction has a similar purpose.

PACE YOURSELF

Think of a movie that you've seen, and write a preview for the movie in the form of an introduction.

The most important component of any introduction is your thesis statement.

What Is a Thesis Statement?

A **thesis statement** is your whole argument, boiled down to a sentence. It serves two functions. One, your thesis allows you to test your argument's strength, by seeing how it holds up to being simplified into one brief statement. Does it end up sounding awkward? Or does it sound like a winner? Two, your thesis introduces the reader to your plan of action and answers that important question that readers ask themselves: *What is the point?*

FUEL FOR THOUGHT

The word *thesis* comes from the Greek word *tithenai*, meaning to put or lay down.

Where Do You Put a Thesis Statement?

In most cases, your thesis statement will go at the end of your introduction. This way, you can build up to it with an intriguing opening. The location of your thesis within the introduction is not nearly as important, however, as the clarity of your thesis statement. Wherever it is, your thesis statement should be clearly identifiable and should make it obvious to your reader what the point of your essay will be.

How Do You Write a Thesis Statement?

Thesis statements are not difficult to write. All you have to do is make sure that you are answering the question you are being asked in your essay assignment. For example, if you are asked to write an essay explaining the major differences between elementary school and middle school, turn that assignment into a question, as follows.

> What are the major differences between elementary school and middle school?

Now your thesis statement will be the answer to the question. It may start like this.

> *The major differences between elementary school and middle school are . . .*

A strong thesis statement will not only answer the question and introduce your point, but it will also take a stand, be specific, and lend itself to further discussion. There's no point in having a thesis statement that doesn't lead to more discussion. After all, that's what your essay is, a discussion of your topic. Let's practice writing some strong thesis statements.

CAUTION!

Don't try to write your thesis after you've written your essay. You'll need to refer back to it as you write.

PRACTICE LAP

Write thesis statements for the following essay topic assignments.

1. Convince your teacher to allow you to work in groups for your next homework assignment.

2. Explain an advantage of being your current age.

3. Describe a time when you helped somebody. Why did you help that person? How did it make you both feel?

Check your answers on page 45.

Now that you've practiced creating some thesis statements, let's take a look at what a good introduction may look like.

> *Many of us love the cold weather. Skiing and snowboarding have become popular recreational activities; others simply enjoy nestling around a warm fire during the winter months. Although winter temperatures can make for a fun time out in the snow or a relaxing day indoors, there are serious dangers associated with cold weather. It is, therefore, important that everyone learns how to stay safe in the cold. There are several ways that a person can keep warm during cold winter months, including dressing in layers, staying indoors, and drinking warm liquids.*

As you can see, this introduction has a clear thesis statement, which appears as the last sentence of the paragraph. There is no confusion as to what the rest of the essay will be about. As we are led up to the thesis, we are given a little bit of background as to why the topic is even being discussed. Why is it important? To whom will this information be helpful? A good introduction will answer these questions for the reader, so that he or she feels there is a good reason to keep reading.

Body

If, in your introduction, you say what you are going to say, then the body of your essay is where you actually say it. Each paragraph of the body of your essay should contain a topic sentence (we'll talk more about topic sentences in a minute) and should serve as direct support for your thesis statement. The body of your paper is where you defend and/or support the point you made in your introduction.

Conclusion

So, in your introduction, you've said what you're going to say. Then, in the body of your essay, you've said it. Now, in your conclusion, you say what you said. This is your chance to remind the reader of your thesis and to sum up your major points. You may want to leave it at that, or you may want to take it a step further and make a recommendation or prediction for the future.

Practice identifying the parts of an essay by dissecting a newspaper article.

TOPIC SENTENCES

We need to consider one other means of organization. Not only your essay as a whole, but also each paragraph within your essay, needs to be organized. So here's the deal. Every paragraph in your essay will have a topic. You will need to introduce that topic to your reader with a topic sentence. A **topic sentence** tells your reader what the paragraph is about, but that's not all the multitalented topic sentence accomplishes. It has to relate simultaneously to your thesis *and* to the rest of the paragraph. Think of the topic sentence as standing tall on the page, holding hands with both the thesis and the paragraph, so that they never get too far apart.

Parts of a Topic Sentence

Because one of the jobs of a topic sentence is to tell your reader what the paragraph is about, it needs to be composed of two important parts: the topic and the focus.

The **topic** is what the paragraph is about. The **focus** is what you think about the topic. Here are some examples of topic sentences with the topic and focus identified.

FOCUS
There are [certain precautions] that a person can take to
TOPIC
(avoid being struck by lightning).

TOPIC FOCUS
People (get sunburns) for a number of [reasons].

TOPIC FOCUS
It is not difficult to (write an essay) if you [follow some simple steps].

PRACTICE LAP

Identify the topic and the focus of the following topic sentences.

4. Many factors contribute to a person being a good driver.

5. Cats make good pets for many reasons.

6. Eating too much candy can be detrimental to your health.

7. There are a number of reasons why carpentry is a rewarding profession.

8. You can prepare yourself for cold weather emergencies by following some simple guidelines.

9. Eating a healthy breakfast can benefit you all day long.

10. Following some simple steps makes it easy to create homemade Valentine cards.

11. Specific atmospheric circumstances must be present in order for it to snow.

Practice writing a topic sentence for each of the following.

12. Topic = protecting your eyes from the sun
    Focus = ways to protect your eyes

13. Topic = running for exercise
    Focus = advantages and disadvantages of running

14. Topic = taking care of potted plants
    Focus = steps to follow

Check your answers on page 46.

KINDS OF PARAGRAPHS

Now that you know how to write a topic sentence that clearly identifies the topic and the focus, let's talk about how to construct the rest of the paragraph. The first decision to make is where to place your topic sentence. Should it be the first sentence, or the last? Or should it be stuck somewhere in the middle? Well, the middle is not an option. Your reader would be very confused to read one of your topic sentences in the middle of a paragraph. The remaining options are putting your topic sentence first or putting it last. Each of these options creates a different type of paragraph. The two types of paragraphs are deductive and inductive.

Deductive Paragraphs

A **deductive** paragraph begins with the topic sentence, so the reader knows right away what the rest of the paragraph will be about. Here's an example.

> *One way to prevent tooth decay is to make regular visits to your dentist. Even if you take care of your teeth every day at home, it is still advantageous to get them cleaned by a dentist a couple of times a year. Brushing, flossing, and using mouthwash at home can clean your teeth only so much. The dentist uses*

special tools that are not available to the average person to use every day on his or her teeth.

Inductive Paragraphs

An **inductive** paragraph ends with the topic sentence and, therefore, is not as straightforward as a deductive paragraph. Instead of introducing the topic right away, the inductive paragraph builds up to introducing the topic. Here's an example.

> *Dentists use special tools to clean your teeth. These tools are not available to most people and clean teeth better than brushing, flossing, and using mouthwash at home. So, in order to supplement your home cleaning, you should visit the dentist a couple times each year. Visiting your dentist regularly is one way to prevent tooth decay.*

For now, don't worry about trying to create inductive paragraphs. Because deductive paragraphs are much more straightforward, they're a good type to start practicing with. After you've had some practice writing essays, you can experiment with different styles.

PRACTICE LAP

15. Now you know about the two kinds of paragraphs and how to create a topic sentence. Using this sample outline as a guide, practice writing a deductive paragraph. Remember that your outline starts generally and gets more specific with each level of information. Use a general idea for your topic sentence and then specifics for the bulk of your paragraph.

I. Recycling can help the environment.
  A. Cuts down on consumer waste
    1. Decreases the number and size of landfills
    2. Decreases the energy and pollution used to transport the waste

B. Not as much production
   1. Production causes pollution.
   2. Uses resources
      a. In the case of paper, production uses trees.
      b. Energy

Check your answers on page 47.

INSIDE TRACK

Details are what make an argument convincing and an essay interesting.

ORGANIZING PARAGRAPHS

Each paragraph of your essay should have a clear topic sentence as the first sentence. Every other sentence should relate back to that topic sentence. It interrupts the flow and the clarity of your essay when there are sentences that seem like they're stuck in the wrong place. Imagine the reader cruising along down the road of your essay and—*pop!*—a pothole! Now, maybe the reader has a flat tire and has to pull over to the shoulder and assess the problem. Sounds like a bummer, huh? That's why flow is so important.

PRACTICE LAP

See if you can identify some out-of-place sentences in the following paragraphs.

16. *My friend and I discovered something new on our day off from school last week. We had gone down to the pond to skip stones, and while we were sitting by the edge of the water, we noticed a tiny little crab coming out of the sand. The last time I was at the beach, I saw crabs and seagulls. Neither of us had seen a crab like that before, and it made us feel like explorers in a faraway land.*

17. *Watching a movie in science class would be a useful supplement to our everyday lessons. Sometimes it helps to step outside the classroom, even if only through a documentary, in order to better understand what we are learning. In math, we are learning about equations. Watching a movie would allow us to experience science in a way that is broader than the classroom allows. We could see examples of concepts that cannot exist in our relatively small room of our relatively small school.*

Check your answers on page 47.

Where to Break

Sometimes it can be tricky trying to decide when to start a new paragraph. Well, each paragraph should contain its own topic, so the rule is new topic, new paragraph. When you're reading back over your essay and find that a paragraph seems to be quite long, maybe it's really two smaller topics that could be broken up into two separate paragraphs.

LET'S RECAP

All this important information will enable you to construct your essay, using your outline as a guide. It is essential to know the basic parts of an essay: an introduction, a body, and a conclusion. First, remember that the introduction is the hook that draws the reader in. You don't want your reader to get stuck in the introduction and not continue on to the body of your paper. Make your introduction clear and interesting, and be sure that you have a well-defined thesis statement so that there's no confusion as to what you will write about in the rest of your essay. Take a stand. Make your point. Tell people what you're about to tell them.

Next is the body of your essay. Generally speaking, you should have at least one paragraph for every piece of support you've gathered for your thesis. Each of these paragraphs should be a mini essay on its own, in the sense that it should discuss only one piece of support and begin with a topic sentence that introduces that support. Of course, each paragraph should also relate directly back to the thesis statement. After reading each paragraph, your reader should be able to say, "Hey, so that's why the thesis is true." Also, as you write, keep in mind the two different kinds of paragraphs. Deductive paragraphs begin with the topic sentence, and inductive paragraphs end with it. Although you'll primarily be using deductive paragraphs because they're much more straightforward and interesting, it's helpful to keep the difference between the two types in mind.

Finally, you will conclude. At this point, you don't want to leave your reader hanging. You want to wrap everything up nicely at the end and remind the reader why your essay was so important to read. Your conclusion should restate your thesis without being repetitive. It should also leave the reader with a little something to think about, whether it be how your topic relates to some larger issue or how it's the very first time anyone has ever discussed the topic. If your essay is a movie and the introduction is the preview, then your conclusion is the nicely wrapped-up happy ending that gives the viewer a good feeling or maybe even something to talk about over dinner.

ANSWERS

1. *We should be allowed to work in groups for our next homework assignment, because it would increase the amount we learn by giving us the opportunity to share knowledge with our classmates.*
   This is an example of a good thesis statement for the given essay topic. If yours is slightly different, that's okay. Just make sure it has all the same basic components. Turning the assignment into a question, it would read something like, "Why should your teacher allow you to work in groups for your next homework assignment?" So, to answer the question and create a thesis statement, you would write, "We should be allowed to work in groups for our next homework assignment, because . . ."
2. *The advantage of being 14 is that I'm old enough to start being independent, but still young enough to have relatively few responsibilities.*
   The question being asked in this assignment is "What are the advantages of your current age?" Whatever you think those advantages are, you should put them into your thesis statement. This is an example of how you could phrase it.
3. *My younger brother needed help with a school project, so I guided him through each step of the process, and we both ended up having a really good time together.*
   This assignment is asking you to talk about a time you helped somebody and how it made you both feel. This is an example of a thesis statement you could create from that assignment. It doesn't matter if you thought of a different answer. What matters is that you restated what you were being asked and included whatever answer you came up with.

4. Topic = being a good driver
   Focus = factors
   The topic is being a good driver, and the focus is the many factors that contribute to being a good driver.
5. Topic = Cats make good pets.
   Focus = reasons
   The topic is cats making good pets, and the reasons why they make good pets is the focus.
6. Topic = eating too much candy
   Focus = detrimental to your health
   Eating too much candy is the topic, and how eating too much candy can be detrimental to your health is the focus.
7. Topic = Carpentry is a rewarding profession.
   Focus = reasons
   The topic is the fact that carpentry is a rewarding profession, and the focus is the reasons why it is a rewarding profession.
8. Topic = prepare yourself for cold weather emergencies
   Focus = simple guidelines
   The topic is preparing for cold weather emergencies, and the focus is the simple guidelines involved in preparing for cold weather.
9. Topic = eating a healthy breakfast
   Focus = benefits
   Eating a healthy breakfast is the topic, and the benefits of eating a healthy breakfast is the focus.
10. Topic = create homemade Valentine cards
    Focus = simple steps
    Creating homemade Valentine cards is the topic, and the simple steps you follow to make those cards is the focus.
11. Topic = snow
    Focus = specific atmospheric circumstances
    Snow is the topic, and the specific atmospheric circumstances that cause snow is the focus.
12. *There are a number of ways you can protect your eyes from the sun.* Your topic sentence may be slightly different in how you phrased it, but as long as you included both the topic and the focus, then your sentence is correct.

13. *Running for exercise has advantages as well as disadvantages.*
You need to state the topic (running for exercise), along with the focus of that topic (advantages and disadvantages).
14. *You can follow some simple steps to take care of your potted plants.*
Your sentence is correct if you included both the topic (taking care of your potted plants) and the focus of that topic (the steps to follow in taking care of your potted plants).
15. *Implementing a recycling program in your school or town is a good step toward helping the environment. The large amount of consumer waste could be decreased by recycling items that we use every day. Decreasing consumer waste would inevitably decrease the number and size of landfills needed to store that waste. Also, the amount of energy used and the pollution caused by transporting consumer waste to landfills would decrease. Therefore, recycling helps the environment not only by decreasing the amount of consumer waste we generate, but by saving the energy used to transport that waste.*
This is an example of a good deductive paragraph that uses the sample outline as a guide. Notice that the topic sentence of the paragraph came from the most general topic you had to work with, which was "Recycling can help the environment." What makes it a deductive paragraph as opposed to an inductive paragraph is that the topic sentence is at the beginning of the paragraph, so the reader knows immediately what the paragraph will be about. The A and B topics in the outline, as well as the examples that support them, are introduced in the paragraph.
16. *The last time I was at the beach, I saw crabs and seagulls.*
Although the paragraph is about noticing a new kind of crab at the pond, it is not relevant that the last time the writer was at the beach, he or she saw crabs and seagulls. It's an interesting piece of information, perhaps, but it doesn't add anything to the meaning of the paragraph as a whole.
17. *In math, we are learning about equations.*
The paragraph is about how watching a movie in science class could be helpful to the learning process. What the writer is learning in math class has nothing to do with the topic at hand, so that sentence is definitely out of place.

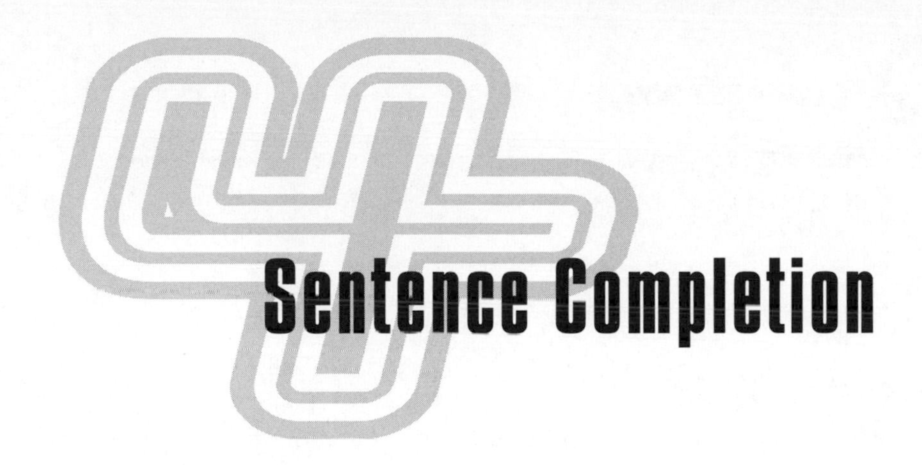

Sentence Completion

One thing is certain. You can't have an essay without sentences. Aside from each individual word, the sentence is the most basic component of any essay. An essay composed of a bunch of lousy sentences is not going to be a good essay. That doesn't mean that if each of your sentences is fabulous, you automatically have an award-winning piece of writing. Of course, there's more to it than that. But the sentence is fundamental. Without sentences, you have no building blocks. You have no way of paving the road for your reader to follow.

WHAT MAKES A SENTENCE COMPLETE?

A complete sentence must have two parts: the subject and the predicate.

The **subject** is what or who the sentence is about, and the **predicate** is what the subject is doing. So, generally speaking, the subject will be a noun and the predicate will be some kind of verb. Here are some sentences with the subject and predicate identified so you can get the idea.

SUBJECT	PREDICATE
[Sally and I]	(went) to the pool.

SUBJECT	PREDICATE
[The cat]	(jumped) onto the fence.

SUBJECT	PREDICATE
[My sister]	(is reading) a science fiction novel.

CAUTION!

More stylized writing will have incomplete sentences, but you shouldn't use them in a formal essay.

PRACTICE LAP

In the following sentences, identify the subject and predicate by putting a box around the subject and circling the predicate.

1. John builds houses for a living.
2. Yesterday, I went to the store with my mom.
3. The fish is swimming around the bowl.
4. I always brush my teeth in the morning and at night.
5. I will eat a sandwich for lunch.
6. We learned how to solve equations in math class.
7. Last summer, my friend Sue went to camp.

Check your answers on page 56.

Sentence Fragments and How to Spot Them

The most common mistake that people make when forming sentences is leaving out either the subject or the predicate. If either the subject or the predicate is left out of a sentence, it's not complete. It's a **sentence fragment**. The good news is, once you are easily able to identify subjects and predicates in sentences, you'll be able to check for sentence fragments in your essay.

PACE YOURSELF

Write a whole paragraph using only sentence fragments. Show it to someone and see if he or she can understand what you wrote.

PRACTICE LAP

See if you can identify which of the following sentences is incomplete.

8. Made a sand castle at the beach.

9. She read a book after school.

10. The dog in the yard.

11. A cup of flour.

12. It is hot in here.

Check your answers on page 57.

SENTENCE COMPLETION QUESTIONS

Some tests you take may have some sentence completion questions that test your vocabulary and logic skills. A sentence completion question gives you a sentence with one or more words missing and then asks you to identify the missing word or words from a list of options. In general, to solve any sentence completion question, you will need to determine what word or words best fit in the given sentence. Don't worry, though. Each question will have clues to help you solve it. Here are the four types of sentence completion questions and some clues for each type.

FUEL FOR THOUGHT

If there are five answer choices and you have to guess, you have a 20% chance of getting it right. If you eliminate one answer, your odds of picking the right answer go up to 25%. Eliminate another and your odds go up to 33.33%. Eliminate yet another and your odds jump to 50%.

Restatement

In this type of question, the word you're looking for is already defined for you in another part of the sentence.

Example

> George was <u>athletic</u>; in fact, he was one of the best players on both his softball team and his basketball team.

Clue phrases: *in fact*, *namely*, *that is*, *in other words*

Being one of best players on both his softball and his basketball team could indicate that George is athletic.

Comparison

In this type of question, two or more things are being compared, so the words are already defined in the sentence.

Example

> Sue received the most votes for class president, and the following year, when her brother ran for the same position, he was also <u>elected</u>.

Clue phrases: *like*, *and*, *just as*, *for example*, *as illustrated by*

Sue's brother had the same experience as Sue, and we know that she received the most votes, which means that she was elected. So, her brother was also elected.

Contrast

In this type of question, two or more things are being contrasted, so the word you are looking for will be the *opposite* of what is defined in the sentence.

Example

Roger was still exhausted, despite having taken a nap earlier in the day.

Clue phrases: *although, however, despite, on the other hand*

In contrast to his napping, which would have made him more energetic, Roger was the opposite of energetic. He was exhausted.

Cause and Effect

In this type of question, the word you are looking for will be either a cause or an effect of what's in the sentence. So, look for either a cause or an effect in the sentence.

Example

As a result of it being so frigid outside, everyone in the park was shivering.

Clue phrases: *therefore, consequently, as a result of, because*

The effect is that everyone in the park was shivering. What caused them to shiver? The frigid temperature caused the shivering.

Let's practice answering a sentence completion question together.

Tommy became ______________ at typing because he practiced every day for five months.

a. dormant
b. valiant
c. proficient
d. reflective
e. redundant

Reading this question, we immediately notice one of the clue words. Tommy became ______________ at typing *because* he practiced every day for five months. It can be helpful to actually say the word *blank* when you are reading the question to yourself. It gives you a filler word, so that the sentence still makes sense to you when you read it. Before you even look at the answer choices, you may want to guess what the missing word could be. This will help you decide what kind of word you are looking for.

So we've noticed our clue word, which lets us know that we're dealing with a cause-and-effect question. Tommy's practicing every day for five months caused him to be what? Which answer makes most sense as the effect of Tommy's practicing? Try out each possible answer as the effect of Tommy's practicing and you'll find that **c** is the best choice. Tommy's practicing made him proficient. To make sure you've selected the correct answer, go back and read the sentence again, filling in each answer choice. That way, you'll be able to hear how the other words don't make sense in the sentence.

Now try some on your own.

INSIDE TRACK

Sometimes it's easier to eliminate than to choose.

PRACTICE LAP

13. The magician ______________ a dove from his empty hands as part of his illusion.
a. decried
b. heralded
c. permeated
d. conjured
e. thwarted

PACE YOURSELF

Using flash cards can increase your vocabulary. Put a word on one side and its definition on the other. Read through the cards every day and have people quiz you.

Here's another way to give your vocabulary a boost: Try doing some crossword puzzles.

14. Samantha needed to speak with her teacher about her test score, because she couldn't believe how much lower it was than the ________________.

a. derivative
b. norm
c. prudence
d. solitude
e. stimulation

15. The police officer was ________________ for finally catching the pickpocket who had been plaguing the town.

a. augmented
b. denigrated
c. mandated
d. lauded
e. reconstituted

Check your answers on page 57.

LET'S RECAP

You can't write an essay without sentences. That's for sure. So what makes a sentence a sentence? You need a subject and a predicate. That's it. Without one or the other, you end up with a sentence fragment. You don't want any sentence fragments in your essay, so it's good to know how to spot them and fix them.

At some point, you will come across sentence completion questions, so it's also good to know how to answer those. There are four types of sentence completion questions: restatement, comparison, contrast, and cause and effect. The good news is that they frequently come with clue words embedded within them, which will help you find your answer. If, for some reason, you can't find a clue word and aren't sure what kind of question you're dealing with, don't worry—just read the sentence saying "blank" instead of the missing word. This will help you hear what the word in the blank should mean based on the rest of the sentence. Go through each answer choice and read the sentence with that answer. Also, remember that it's always easier to eliminate incorrect answers than to choose a correct one, so if you can eliminate a choice as incorrect, do it!

ANSWERS

1. [John] (builds) houses for a living.
   The subject of the sentence is *John*. What does John do? John builds, so *builds* is the predicate.
2. Yesterday, [I] (went) to the store with my mom.
   I is the subject of the sentence, and what did *I* do? I went, so *went* is the predicate.
3. [The fish] (is swimming) around the bowl.
   The fish is the subject of the sentence, and what is the fish doing? The fish is swimming, so *is swimming* is the predicate.
4. [I] always (brush) my teeth in the morning and at night.
   I is the subject of the sentence, and what do I do? I brush, so *brush* is the predicate.
5. [I] (will eat) a sandwich for lunch.
   I is the subject of the sentence, and what will I do? I will eat, so *will eat* is the predicate.
6. [We] (learned) how to solve equations in math class.
   We is the subject of the sentence. What did we do? We learned, so *learned* is the predicate.
7. Last summer, my friend [Sue] (went) to camp.
   The subject of the sentence is *Sue*. What did Sue do? Sue went, so the predicate of the sentence is *went*.

8. incomplete
Made a sand castle at the beach is lacking a subject, so it is incomplete. Who made a sand castle at the beach? That information needs to be included in order for the sentence to be complete.

9. complete
This sentence has a subject and a predicate and is, therefore, complete. The subject is *she*, and she read, so *read* is the predicate.

10. incomplete
The dog in the yard is incomplete because it is lacking a predicate. What is the dog doing in the yard? *The dog* is the subject. We just need to know what the dog is doing.

11. incomplete
A cup of flour is not a complete sentence, because we don't know what the cup of flour is doing or what someone else may be doing with the cup of flour. The *cup of flour* is the subject, but there is no predicate, so the sentence is incomplete.

12. complete
This is a complete sentence, because there is a subject and a predicate. The subject is *it*, and the predicate is *is*. *It is*: That's a complete sentence in and of itself.

13. **d.** We know that whatever fits in the blank is something that the magician did to the dove, and we know that it was an illusion. Based on the meanings of each of the five answer choices, *conjured* is the best choice to fill in the blank. To *conjure* means to summon or call up. It makes sense that if the magician summoned a dove from his empty hands, it would be considered an illusion.

14. **b.** *Norm* is the only word that makes sense in the sentence. The norm is the average, so Samantha needed to speak with her teacher because she couldn't believe that her score was below the average.

15. **d.** To *laud* someone means to praise him or her, so *lauded* is the best fit for the blank in the sentence. You know that the police officer did something good by catching the pickpocket. So, doing something good would result in what? It would result in the officer being praised.

Grammar

I know. Grammar, yuck. But eliminating grammatical errors from your writing is one of the single most effective things you can do to improve it. We've talked about how important sentences are to our final essay, and poor grammar is a good way to make a bad sentence.

WHEN A GOOD SENTENCE GOES BAD

Here are some common grammatical errors. Keep them on your radar screen.

Subject/Verb Agreement

This is exactly how it sounds. The subject and the verb of the sentence don't agree. In a correct sentence, if the subject (or noun) is singular, then the verb should be a singular form of that verb. In the following example of an incorrect sentence, *Jim* is a singular subject, and *wash* is a plural form, so the sentence doesn't make sense.

> *Jim wash* the car.

Many people *wash* a car, but one person *washes* a car. Here are two correct ways to write the sentence.

Jim washes the car.
Jim and his friends wash the car.

Verb Tense Shift

Make sure that the verb tense is consistent throughout each sentence.

Sally *went* to the store and *buys* carrots.

If Sally went to the store in the past tense, then she also bought carrots in the past tense. She didn't buy them now if she went to the store in the past. The trick is to make sure that everything that occurred in the past is expressed with a verb in the past tense and vice versa. The sentence should be written like this.

Sally *went* to the store and *bought* carrots.

Here's another example of a verb tense shift error, along with the appropriate corrections.

We *go* to the pool and *swam*.	[incorrect]
We *go* to the pool and *swim*.	[correct]
We *went* to the pool and *swam*.	[correct]

The Past Participle

A **past participle** form of a verb is when the action verb is combined with a helping verb, like *has* or *have*. The past participle forms of regular verbs are the same as the past tense form of that same verb. For instance, the past tense of *smile* is *smiled*. It is a regular verb, so the past participle of *smile* is *has smiled*. The same is true with the verb *cook*. The past tense is *cooked* and the past participle is *has cooked*. Here is an example of how you can make a mistake using the past participle of a regular verb.

The caterpillar *has turn* into a butterfly.	[incorrect]
The caterpillar *has turned* into a butterfly.	[correct]

The past participle form of irregular verbs is a little bit different. Irregular verbs change forms in the past tense. Although there are many, here are a few so you get the idea of which words we're talking about.

sleep/slept
eat/ate
teach/taught
catch/caught
run/ran
sit/sat

These verbs are tricky in the past participle form because they aren't as straightforward as the regular verbs. Here are the same verbs in past participle form.

slept/has slept
ate/has eaten
taught/has taught
caught/has caught
ran/has run
sat/has sat

As you can see, some of the irregular verbs stay the same in past participle with only the addition of the helping verb. Others (like *ate* and *ran*) take on a version of the present tense. Here is an example of a mistake you could make with the past participle of an irregular verb.

It has been so cold that all the puddles *have froze*. [incorrect]
It has been so cold that all the puddles *have frozen*. [correct]

The verb *freeze* is an irregular verb whose past tense form is *froze*. But when used in the past participle form, an *n* is added to make the word *frozen*. Be careful with these words. They're tricky.

Run-On Sentences/Comma Splices

Make sure you're not combining two sentences in an incorrect way. Sometimes, without realizing it, you may make the mistake of combining two sentences, when they should either be entirely separate sentences or be linked with correct punctuation. The following incorrect sentence is really two distinct sentences.

> Summer isn't over it's only July.

The two distinct sentences are *Summer isn't over* and *It's only July*. To fix the error, you could either add a period after *over* and capitalize the *I* of *it's* to make them separate, like this:

> Summer isn't over. It's only July.

or you could insert a semicolon, as follows:

> Summer isn't over; it's only July.

Semicolons are used to connect two otherwise independent sentences whose meanings relate to each other in a close way. It would be incorrect to do this:

> I like summer, it's so hot.

You cannot fix the sentence by simply inserting a comma between the two sentences. There is another way that you can correct a run-on sentence. You can create a dependent clause, as follows:

> I like summer because it's so hot.

FUEL FOR THOUGHT

A **dependent clause** is a group of words that has a subject and a predicate but does not express a complete thought.

PACE YOURSELF

Rewrite a newspaper article without any punctuation. See if you can correctly add the punctuation back in yourself.

Pronouns

A **pronoun** is a word that replaces a noun in a sentence. Sometimes knowing which pronoun to use can be complicated, especially when replacing nouns other than proper names. Take a look at this incorrect sentence.

Everyone has *their* favorite food.

Everyone is singular, even though it seems plural. Think of it as *every one person*. *Their* is plural, so the two don't go together. The correct way to write this sentence follows.

Everyone has *his or her* favorite food.

Here is a list of some other pronouns that seem plural but are really singular. Each would need to be used with another singular pronoun, such as *his* or *her*.

nobody
everybody
no one
each
somebody
either
anyone

Pronouns can also get confusing when they are paired with *I* or *me*. For instance, the following sentence is incorrect.

Her and me went to the mall.

An easy way to see which pronoun to use in a sentence is to test them individually. See if either *her* or *me* makes sense in the sentence by itself. It would be incorrect to say, *Her went to the mall*, and it would also be incorrect to say, *Me went to the mall*. So, together, they don't make sense. To be correct, you would say, *I went to the mall* or *She went to the mall*, so the sentence should read as follows.

She and I went to the mall.

So, if you're facing a pair of pronouns and are unsure which to use, just read the sentence with only one pronoun at a time to figure it out.

Apostrophes

Apostrophes are used either to show possession or to combine two words together in a contraction. To show possession for a singular noun, an apostrophe and an *s* are added. Here's an example.

Danny's shoe is untied.

For a plural noun, the rule is slightly different. If a noun is plural, you put the apostrophe after the *s*, as in this example.

His *parents'* friends were over for dinner.

Here's another example of a plural noun that is made possessive by adding an *s* and an apostrophe.

> The *clouds'* colors were amazing shades of purple.

Then, there's also the *it* rule. The rule for *it* is that, to make *it* possessive, just add an *s* but no apostrophe. *It's* is used only as a contraction for *it is*. Here is an example of an incorrect sentence, followed by the corrected version.

The dog was licking *it's* paw.	[incorrect]
The dog was licking *its* paw.	[correct]

CAUTION!

Never use *its'*.

Commas

Commas are basically used as dividers. There are four instances in which commas are commonly forgotten. One of these instances involves a series or list. In this example, commas are being used to divide a list of various items.

We need *apples oranges and bananas.*	[incorrect]
We need *apples, oranges, and bananas.*	[correct]

INSIDE TRACK

Commas are usually needed at the points in the sentence when someone may pause when reading, so read the sentence out loud to see where you pause.

Commas are needed after an introductory clause, but are often forgotten. An introductory clause sets up the situation for the sentence, so it needs to be separated from the rest of the sentence with a comma. Take the following incorrect sentence.

Because I didn't have my key I couldn't get into my house.

Because I didn't have my key sets up the situation of not being able to get into the house, so it needs to be separated by a comma, like this:

Because I didn't have my key, I couldn't get into my house.

The same is true in the following example; here, there are two independent clauses.

The weather fascinates him
so he wants to be a meteorologist. [incorrect]
The weather fascinates him,
so he wants to be a meteorologist. [correct]

Commas are also sometimes left out of a nonrestrictive clause. A **nonrestrictive clause** is a part of the sentence that is nonessential. For example, read the following incorrect sentence.

Nancy's pencil *which is yellow* just fell onto the floor.

Which is yellow is not essential to the sentence. It is an aside, so it needs to be set apart with commas. Here's the correct way to write the sentence.

Nancy's pencil, *which is yellow,* just fell onto the floor.

Misplaced Modifiers

A **modifier** is a part of the sentence that describes or provides more detail. A modifier is misplaced if it is not clear which part of the sentence it is modifying. For example, the following sentence is incorrect.

I was stung by a bee *walking in the park*.

It is unclear who was walking in the park, *I* or the *bee*.

This corrected sentence clears up any confusion over who was walking in the park.

When I was walking in the park, I was stung by a bee.

INSIDE TRACK

If you're not sure if there's a misplaced modifier in a sentence, ask yourself the question, Who is doing what? You should be able to answer without hesitation.

PRACTICE LAP

Identify the following sentences as correct or incorrect.

1. My friend and I like to go down by the lake and played catch.
2. Joe and me share the same sense of humor.
3. Because I love dogs, I want to adopt one from the shelter.
4. Roger laughs at the joke, because he thinks its funny.
5. The cat was licking its face.
6. The movie hasn't started yet it's still the opening credits.
7. It was raining so hard that everyone had gone indoors.

Rewrite the following incorrect sentences to fix the grammatical mistakes.

8. At four years old, my mother taught me how to tie my shoes.

9. I'm reading a funny book it makes me laugh out loud.

10. All of the plants pots are made out of plastic.

11. Everyone put on their coat before they left.

12. Because its getting dark outside Bill and me decide to head home.

13. The chicken could have been hit by a truck crossing the road.

14. My parent's made my brother and I dinner.

15. The mans umbrella was losing its shape in the wind.

Check your answers on page 69.

LET'S RECAP

Many people are intimidated by grammar, but just like writing an essay, if you break grammar down into common mistakes and learn how to fix them one at a time, eliminating grammatical errors isn't such a daunting task. Here is a review of eight of the most common grammatical errors.

1. Subject/Verb Agreement

If the subject is singular, the verb must be singular. If the subject is plural, the verb must be plural.

2. Verb Tense Shift

Make sure everything that happened in the past is expressed in the past tense. The same rule holds true with the present tense.

3. The Past Participle

The past participle is the tense of a verb that uses a helping verb such as *has* or *have*. Just remember to be aware of how the verb may need to change in this tense, especially irregular verbs.

4. Run-On Sentences/Comma Splices

Be careful that you don't combine two sentences in an incorrect way. Separate them with periods or semicolons.

5. Pronouns

When grouping pronouns, make sure you're pairing the right ones together. Read the sentence with one pronoun at a time to determine the correct pronouns to use.

6. Apostrophes

Be aware of whether a word is possessive or a contraction. And remember the "it" rule. *Its* is possessive, and *it's* is a contraction for *it is*.

7. Commas

Use commas as dividers, between items in a list, after introductory clauses, between two independent clauses, and around a nonrestrictive clause.

8. Misplaced Modifiers

Make sure it is clear what action the subject is performing in the sentence.

After some practice, all eight of these grammatical issues will become second nature to you. You won't even have to think about them. It'll just start to sound strange to you when you read a sentence that's incorrect.

Remember that grammatical errors can do a lot of damage to an otherwise flawless essay. Don't let them bring you down.

ANSWERS

1. incorrect
   There is a verb tense shift in this sentence. The first part of the sentence says *My friend and I like*, while the second part of the sentence says

played. The sentence should read, *My friend and I like to go down by the lake and* play *catch*.

2. incorrect

If you read the sentence with each subject individually, you'll see that Joe can share something, but *me* cannot share something. *I* share something. To be correct, the sentence should read, *Joe and* I *share the same sense of humor*.

3. correct

Because I love dogs is an introductory clause and is, therefore, correctly offset by a comma at the beginning of the sentence.

4. incorrect

The comma in the sentence is in the correct place, but the *its* at the end of the sentence is incorrect. *Its* without an apostrophe is possessive, and in this case, it is supposed to be used as a contraction for *it is*. So it should be *it's*, instead of *its*. The sentence should read, *Roger laughs at the joke, because he thinks* it's *funny*.

5. correct

In this case, *its* is used correctly to indicate the possessive form. The face belongs to the cat.

6. incorrect

This is a run-on sentence. These two completely separate sentences need to be separated by either a period or a semicolon. It would be correct to write it as *The movie hasn't started yet; it's still the opening credits.*

7. correct

This sentence contains the past participle of the verb *to go*. *Go* is an irregular verb and changes form when used as a past participle. *Had gone* is the correct past participle form of the verb.

8. *When I was four years old, my mother taught me how to tie my shoes.*

This sentence has a misplaced modifier. It is unclear who was four years old, *me* or *my mother*. By saying *when I was four years old*, the confusion is eliminated.

9. *I'm reading a funny book; it makes me laugh out loud.*

This is a run-on sentence and needs to be divided. The semicolon separates the two distinct thoughts.

10. *All of the plants' pots are made out of plastic.*
Plants is meant to be possessive in the sentence. Because *plants* is plural and we're talking about the pots belonging to *all* of the plants, the apostrophe needs to go after the *s*.

11. *Everyone put on his or her coat before he or she left.*
Everyone is singular. It is the same as saying *every one person*. And every one person puts on *his or her* coat, not *their* coat. So *their* and *they* in the sentence both need to be changed to the singular forms of the pronoun: *his/her* and *he/she*.

12. *Because it's getting dark outside, Bill and I decide to head home.*
This sentence has three errors. One is *its*. In this case, *its* should be used as a contraction for *it is*, not a possessive, so *it's* is correct. The second error is the missing comma after the introductory clause. *Because it's dark outside* sets up the rest of the sentence and needs to be set apart. The third error is the pronoun in the phrase *Bill and me*. You wouldn't say, *Because it's getting dark outside, me decide to head home*. That doesn't make sense. You'd say, *I decide to head home*. So the sentence should read *Bill and I*.

13. *When crossing the road, the chicken could have been hit by a truck.*
This is another case of a misplaced modifier that confuses the meaning of the sentence. The incorrect version makes it seem as if the truck, not the chicken, were crossing the road. By rewriting the sentence to create an introductory clause, you can make the meaning much clearer.

14. *My parents made my brother and me dinner.*
This sentence has two errors. One is the apostrophe in *parent's*. This word is meant to be not possessive, but plural, so it does not need an apostrophe. The other error is the pronoun in the phrase *my brother and I*. The phrase should read *my brother and me*, because my parents would make *me* dinner. They wouldn't make *I* dinner.

15. *The man's umbrella was losing its shape in the wind.*
In this sentence, *mans* should be possessive, because the umbrella belongs to the man. To make *mans* possessive, you need to add an apostrophe after *man*. The pronoun *its* is correct as is in the sentence.

Tricky Words

The English language can be tricky. Many words sound the same but have completely different meanings. In some cases, you have to change only a single letter of a word to make it mean something entirely new. How confusing is that? Here is a list of some commonly misused, misspelled, or confused words.

CONFUSED WORDS AND PHRASES

a lot (noun):	many or much
allot (verb):	to give or share

CAUTION!

Alot is not a word.

accept (verb):	to recognize or allow
except (preposition):	excluding

FUEL FOR THOUGHT

A **preposition** is a word that tells the relationship between nouns in a sentence (for example, *The cat sat* under *the table*).

access (noun, verb): means of approaching; to approach
excess (noun, adj.): extra

addition (noun): an increase
edition (noun): an issue of a book or newspaper

affect (verb): to influence or change
effect (noun): a result
effect (verb): to bring about

all ready (adj.): completely prepared
already (adv.): by or before a specified or implied time

all together (adj.): in a group; in unison
altogether (adv.): completely or thoroughly

allude (verb): to refer to something not specifically mentioned
elude (verb): to escape notice or detection

ascent (noun): the act of climbing or rising
assent (verb): to agree or accept a proposal or opinion

assure (verb): to reinforce an idea; to comfort someone
ensure (verb): to make certain that something happens
insure (verb): to secure from harm; to secure life or property in case of loss

beside (adj.):	next to
besides (adv.):	in addition to
bibliography (noun):	a list of publications used as reference
biography (noun):	a life story
capital (noun):	money invested; a town or city where the government is located
capitol (noun):	a government building
choose (verb):	to select
chose (verb):	the past tense of *choose*
cite (verb):	to acknowledge; to quote as a reference
sight (noun):	the ability to see; vision
site (noun):	a place or location
complement (noun, verb):	a match for something; to enhance or go well with something
compliment (noun, verb):	praise; to give praise
consul (noun):	an official appointed by the government to live in a foreign country and attend to the interests of the official's home country
council (noun):	a group of people called together to provide advice or govern
counsel (noun, verb):	advice; to give advice
continual (adj.):	taking place in close succession
continuous (adj.):	without a break or letting up
cooperation (noun):	assistance, help
corporation (noun):	type of business organization

CAUTION!

The expression is *I couldn't care less*, not *I could care less.* Many people say it wrong. Listen to see if you can hear when people use it incorrectly.

decent (adj.):	well mannered
descent (noun):	decline, fall
dissent (noun):	disagreement
desert (noun, verb):	arid, sandy region; to abandon or withdraw from
dessert (noun):	a sweet food served at the end of a meal
disburse (verb):	to pay
disperse (verb):	to spread out
disinterested (adj.):	no strong opinion either way; objective, neutral
uninterested (adj.):	don't care; bored
elicit (verb):	to stir up; to call for (responses)
illicit (adj.):	illegal
envelop (verb):	to surround; to cover completely
envelope (noun):	a flat paper container for letters or other documents
farther (adv.):	beyond
further (adj.):	additional

INSIDE TRACK

Use *farther* when referring to actual distance and *further* when referring to nonmeasurable subjects: *I have* farther *to walk and* further *to discuss.*

forth (adv.):	forward, onward
fourth (adj.):	next number after third
hear (verb):	to perceive by the ear
here (adv.):	in or at this place
hoard (verb):	to collect and keep
horde (noun):	a huge crowd
imply (verb):	to hint or suggest (to someone)
infer (verb):	to assume or deduce (from someone)
loose (adj.):	not restrained, not fastened
lose (verb):	to fail to win; to be deprived of
loath (adj.):	reluctant
loathe (verb):	to feel hatred for
medal (noun):	a badge of honor
meddle (verb):	to interfere
metal (noun):	a mineral substance
passed (verb):	the past tense of *to pass*
past (adj.):	finished; gone by
personal (adj.):	individual
personnel (noun):	employees

principal (adj.):	main
principal (noun):	person in charge; a sum of money earning interest
principle (noun):	a rule to live by
quiet (adj.):	still, calm
quit (verb):	to stop; to discontinue
quite (adv.):	very, fairly, positively
stationary (adj.):	not moving
stationery (noun):	writing paper

INSIDE TRACK

When trying to distinguish between *stationary* and *stationery*, think of *E* for *envelope* (what stationery goes in) and *A* for *stand still* (what you do when you're stationary).

taught (verb):	the past tense of *to teach*
taut (adj.):	tight
than (conj., prep.):	in contrast to
then (adv.):	next
their (pronoun):	belonging to them
there (adv.):	in a place
they're:	contraction for *they are*
to (prep.):	in the direction of
too (adv.):	also; excessively
two (adj.):	the number after one
weather (noun, verb):	atmospheric conditions; to last or ride out
whether (conj.):	if it be the case; in either case

who (pronoun): substitute for *he*, *she*, or *they*
whom (pronoun): substitute for *him*, *her*, or *them*

your (pronoun): belonging to you
you're: contraction for *you are*

FUEL FOR THOUGHT

Flammable and *inflammable* mean the same thing. They both mean capable of being burned quickly.

MISUSED WORDS

amount: use when you cannot count the items to which you are referring and when referring to singular nouns (for example, *the amount of sunlight in the room*)
number: use when you can count the items to which you are referring and when referring to plural nouns (for example, *the number of stars in the sky*)

anxious: use to mean nervous
eager: use to mean enthusiastic or looking forward to something

among: use when comparing or referring to three or more people or things
between: use when comparing or referring to just two people or things

can: use to state ability
may: use to state permission

PACE YOURSELF

Listen to people around you to hear how correctly, or often incorrectly, they use tricky words.

each other: use when referring to just two people or things
one another: use when referring to three or more people or things

e.g.: use as an abbreviation for the Latin phrase *exempli gratia*, meaning *free example* or *for example*
i.e.: use as an abbreviation for the Latin phrase *id est*, meaning *it is* or *that is*

feel bad: use when talking about physical ailments
feel badly: use when talking about emotional stress

fewer: use when you can count items (for example, *The bucket holds* fewer *quarts of water*.)
less: use when you cannot count the items (for example, *That bucket holds* less *water*.)

PACE YOURSELF

Decide whether you'd use *fewer* or *less* with each of these words.

groceries
orange juice
fingers
skin
time
trees
grass

good:	adjective that describes a person, place, or thing
well:	adverb that describes an action or verb
its:	belonging to *it*
it's:	contraction of *it is*
lay:	to place an item somewhere (for example, *I* lay *the books on the table.*)
lie:	to recline or be placed (for example, *The books* lie *on the table.*)
that:	pronoun that introduces a restrictive clause
which:	pronoun that introduces a nonrestrictive clause

PACE YOURSELF

Make spelling flash cards. Put one word on each card and have someone quiz you twice a week.

COMMONLY MISSPELLED WORDS

absence
abundance
accidentally
accommodate
acknowledgment
acquaintance
aggravate
alibi
alleged
ambiguous
analysis
annual
argument
awkward
basically
boundary
bulletin
calendar
canceled
cannot
cemetery
coincidence
committee
comparative
completely
condemn
congratulations
conscientious
consistent
convenient
correspondence
deceive
definitely
dependent
depot
descend

desperate
development
dilemma
discrepancy
eighth
eligible
embarrass
equivalent
euphoria
existence
exuberance
feasible
February
fifth
forcibly
forfeit
formerly
fourth
fulfill
grateful
grievance
guarantee
guidance
harass
hindrance
ideally
implement
independence
indispensable
inoculate
insufficient
interrupt
jealousy
jewelry
judgment
leisure
length
lenient
liaison
lieutenant
lightning
loophole
losing
maintenance
maneuver
mathematics
millennium
minuscule
miscellaneous
misspell
negotiable
ninth
occasionally
occurred
omission
opportunity
outrageous
pamphlet
parallel
perceive
permanent
perseverance
personnel
possess
potato
precede
preferred
prejudice
prevalent
privilege
procedure
proceed
prominent
pronunciation
quandary
questionnaire
receipt
receive
recommend
reference
referred
regardless
relevant
religious
remembrance
reservoir
responsible
restaurant
rhythm
ridiculous
roommate
scary
scissors
secretary
separate
souvenir
specifically
sufficient
supersede
temperament
temperature
truly
twelfth
ubiquitous
usually
usurp
vacuum
vengeance
visible
Wednesday
wherever

INSIDE TRACK

Keep a dictionary handy. If you don't know how to spell something, look it up, or go online to find out.

PRACTICE LAP

Circle the correctly spelled word in each sentence.

1. I don't even want to think about it, because I (could/couldn't) care less.
2. She has two (less/fewer) cookies (then/than) I have.
3. I feel (bad/badly) about the way I was treated.
4. Chris is tired and wants to (lay/lie) down.
5. (May/can) I ask who is calling?
6. The members of the baseball team sometimes had arguments (between/among) them.
7. To help them eat (their/they're/there) carrots, rabbits have (to/too/two) big front teeth.
8. My friend (implied/inferred) that I should get her a gift for her birthday, so I (implied/inferred) that she wants me to get her one.
9. How much (further/farther) are we going to walk?
10. Sometimes it can be (quiet/quite/quit) difficult to be (quiet/quite/quit) in the library.

11. For my letter, I'm going to need a piece of (stationary/stationery) and an (envelop/envelope).

12. My dad likes having pie for (desert/dessert).

13. My uncle is a member of the town (counsel/consul/council) and works in the (capital/capitol).

14. (Beside/besides) having a younger brother, he also has a younger sister.

15. My parents (assured/ensured/insured) our house to (assure/ensure/insure) that we would be okay if anything happened to it.

LET'S RECAP

The English language is complicated. Many words sound the same and are spelled similarly, but have completely different meanings. One of your goals in writing your essay is to express yourself clearly, and knowing the right words to use is an essential part of reaching that goal.

Take some time to learn the words in this chapter so that when you come across them in your writing, you'll know exactly what they mean and how to use them in a sentence. Your essay will be stronger in the end.

ANSWERS

1. couldn't
If you *could* care less, then you care some, and if you don't even want to think about it, you probably don't care.

2. fewer . . . than
Because you can count individual cookies, you would use *fewer* instead of *less*. *Than* is used to make a comparison, whereas *then* refers to a place in time.

3. badly
When referring to emotions, use *badly*, not *bad*.

4. lie

   Lie is to recline or be placed, while *lay* is the action of placing something. Chris wants to recline, not to place something.

5. may

   May is asking for permission. You wouldn't ask the person on the phone if you were capable of asking who was calling. You would be asking the person's permission to find out who was calling.

6. among

   There are more than two members of a baseball team, so *among* should be used.

7. their . . . two

   Their is possessive and should be used to indicate that the carrots belong to the rabbits. *Two* is the number of big front teeth that they have.

8. implied . . . inferred

   When someone *implies* something, he or she hints at it, and when another person *infers* something, he or she assumes it. The friend *implied* that she wanted a gift, so the writer *inferred* that he should get one.

9. farther

   Farther refers to actual distance, whereas *further* refers to the addition of something. In this case, we are walking a distance, so *farther* is the correct word to use.

10. quite . . . quiet

    Quite means fairly or relatively, so it makes sense in the first part of the sentence. *Quiet* is the correct word for the second part. The other words don't make sense in the sentence.

11. stationery . . . envelope

    Stationery with an *e*, not *stationary* with an *a*, refers to a piece of paper on which you write. *Envelope* is a noun used to mail stationery, while *envelop* is a verb and, therefore, doesn't make sense in this context.

12. dessert

A person eats pie for *dessert*, which is the sweet course at the end of a meal. A *desert* is a hot, arid region. You can remember that *dessert* has two *s*'s because everyone wants two helpings of dessert!

13. council . . . capitol

The town *council* is a governing body, and the *capitol* is an actual government building, not the city in which that building resides.

14. besides

Beside refers to the location of something, whereas *besides* is another way of saying *in addition to*. In the sentence, you could replace *besides* with *in addition to*, so that the sentence reads, *In addition to having a younger brother, he also has a younger sister.*

15. insured . . . ensure

To *insure* something means to secure it from harm. To *ensure* means to make certain. The parents secured the house from harm to make certain that the family would be okay.

7 Passive Voice versus Active Voice

In writing, the term *voice* is often used to refer to the particular way that you are expressing your thoughts and ideas. Just like when you talk, when you write, you have a unique voice. Without even realizing it, you may alter your voice based on what you are writing and to whom you are writing. For instance, you would not use the same voice to write a letter to the president as you would to write an e-mail to your friend. You would use a more informal voice when writing to your friend.

PACE YOURSELF

For fun, trying writing a paragraph in someone else's voice, such as a friend's or even a pet's.

Most of the time, we aren't aware of what type of voice we are using. It just comes out naturally. However, just as the formality of your voice has an effect on your final product, so does whether your voice is *active* or *passive*. Often, active and passive voices are used incorrectly in writing. Let's learn what these voices are and when to use them, so that the voice in your writing can be as strong and as clear as possible.

ACTIVE VOICE

What Is It?

In **active voice**, the subject of the sentence *does* the action of the sentence. For instance, look at this sentence.

Bob *is walking* the dog.

Bob is the subject of the sentence. *Walking the dog* is what is being done in the sentence. Who is walking the dog? Bob is walking the dog. So, the subject (*Bob*) is the one who is doing the action (*walking the dog*).

Here's another example.

You always *laugh* at my jokes.

You is the subject. *Laugh* is the action. Who laughs? You laugh.

PASSIVE VOICE

What Is It?

In **passive voice**, the subject of the sentence *receives* the action of the sentence. Let's go back to Bob and his dog for a second. Here's what that sentence would look like if it were written in passive voice.

The dog *is being walked* by Bob.

This time, the subject of the sentence is *the dog*, but the action is still the same. The action is *being walked*, but Bob is the one who is *doing* the action. Bob is walking the dog. In this case, the dog is *receiving* the action.

Here's another sentence written in passive voice.

The pool *was cleaned* by Janice.

The subject of the sentence is the *pool*. The action of the sentence is *the cleaning of the pool*. Who is doing the cleaning? Janice, not the pool, is doing the cleaning. The pool is *receiving* the action, which is why the sentence is passive. If we rewrote the sentence using the active voice, it would sound much better.

Janice *cleaned* the pool.

CAUTION!

Sometimes people use passive voice because they think it's more formal. Avoid using it, even in formal writing.

The passive voice is also used in cases in which the subject that is *doing* the verb is unknown. Here's an example.

My car *was stolen.*

My car is the subject of the sentence, and *the stealing of the car* is the action of the sentence. The car *receives* the action. Because who did the stealing is unknown, it is acceptable to write the sentence in the passive voice. If it turns out that a man named Richard stole the car, then the sentence could be written in active voice, like this:

Richard *stole* my car.

INSIDE TRACK

Ask yourself who or what the sentence is supposed to be about. Is the subject of the sentence who or what you intended?

Which Voice to Use

Unless it's absolutely necessary, as in the case of the stolen car, you should stick with the active voice is in your writing. Because the action is always being done by the subject is the sentence, the active voice is a much more direct way of saying things. Passive voice can be wordy and vague, and if used too often in one piece of writing, it begins to sound very dull. Take the following sentence that's meant to sound exciting.

My favorite superhero saved the world!

What if it were written in passive voice?

The world was saved by my favorite superhero!

It just doesn't have the same ring to it, does it?

PACE YOURSELF

Write a paragraph describing your day. Use only passive voice.

PRACTICE LAP

Identify whether the following sentences are written in the *passive* or *active* voice.

1. The doctor gave me a shot so that I wouldn't get sick.
2. Caroline rode her bike to school.
3. The mail was delivered around noon today.
4. Halfway through the picnic, I was stung on my foot.
5. The grocery store clerk handed me my change.

6. My father taught me how to surf.

7. Camels store water in their humps.

8. I was given a birthday gift.

The following sentences are all written in the *active* voice. Rewrite each one in the *passive* voice.

9. Suzy showed me the painting.

10. Ben took a photograph of his dog.

11. I washed the dishes this morning.

The following sentences are all written in the *passive* voice. Rewrite them using the *active* voice.

12. My meal was served to me by the waiter at the restaurant.

13. The trash was collected by the janitor.

14. Footprints were made in the snow by me.

Check your answers on page 92.

LET'S RECAP

The passive and active voices are aspects of writing that are always present, but we don't necessarily pay much attention to them. We go about our lives, reading and writing, and we rarely stop to think about whether what we are reading or writing is in the passive or active voice. It does make a big difference, though, in how we perceive what we are reading.

Using the passive voice is an indirect way of saying something because it makes the receiver of the action in the sentence the main subject. If you use it repeatedly, your writing will sound rather weak. The active voice, on the other hand, is much more direct because the subject in the sentence is the one performing the action. You could say, "Lunch was made by me," but doesn't that seem awkward? Why wouldn't you just say, "I made lunch?" Do you see the difference? So, get to know the passive voice and active voice. That way, when you're writing, you'll know how to make your essay sound best to a reader.

ANSWERS

1. active
   The subject of the sentence is the one performing the action. The doctor gave the shot.
2. active
   Caroline is the subject, and she is the one who rode the bike.
3. passive
   This sentence is written in the passive voice, because we know that the mail was delivered, but we don't know *who* delivered it.
4. passive
   This sentence is written in the passive voice, because the subject of the sentence is the recipient of the action of the sentence.
5. active
   The clerk is performing the action of the sentence by handing me my change, so the sentence is written in the active voice.
6. active
   Who did the teaching? *My father* did, so the sentence is written in the active voice.
7. active
   The camels are the subject of the sentence, and they are doing the storing, so the sentence is written in the active voice.
8. passive
   This sentence is written in the passive voice, because the subject of the sentence is receiving the action of the sentence. *I* is the subject, and *I was given* a gift.
9. I was shown the painting.
   Instead of *Suzy* being the subject of the sentence, now *I* is the subject and receives the action instead of performing it.

10. A photograph was taken of Ben's dog.
    In the active voice version of this sentence, we knew that Ben was the one who took the photograph. He was the subject of the sentence. Now, in the passive voice version, the photograph is the subject, and it is receiving the action. We aren't sure anymore who took the photograph.
11. This morning, the dishes were washed.
    I was the subject in the original sentence. Now the subject is the dishes, and the action is happening to them.
12. At the restaurant, the waiter served me my meal.
    Instead of the meal being the subject of the sentence and receiving the action of the sentence, in the active voice version, the waiter is the subject and performs the action.
13. The janitor collected the trash.
    Now, in the active voice version of the sentence, the janitor is the subject of the sentence and also performs the action of the sentence. He collected the trash.
14. I made footprints in the snow.
    In the active voice, *I* is the subject of the sentence and also performs the action of making footprints.

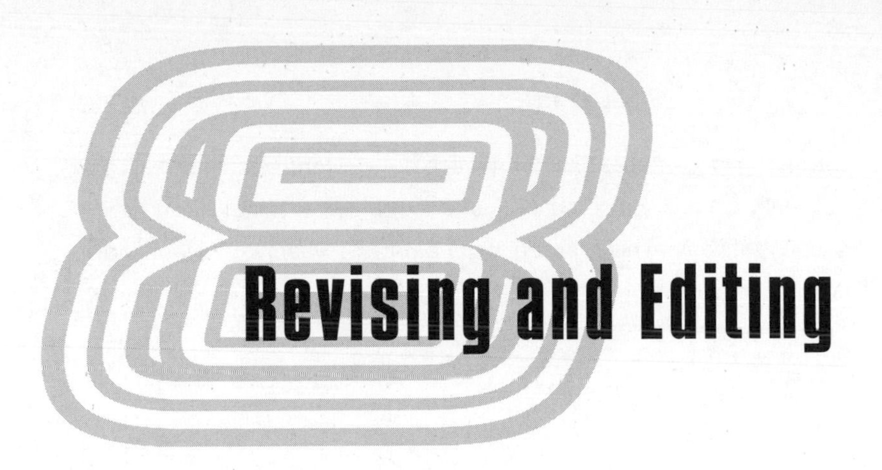

Revising and Editing

So, *you've* written your essay. It's all printed out, with your name on it and everything. You're glad that you're done. But wait! You're not done! It's tempting to stop at this point and turn in your essay as it is. You've worked hard to create a clear piece of writing, with well-thought-out points and well-constructed paragraphs. You'd be amazed, however, at how much your essay can improve with a little revising and editing.

FRESH EYES

Don't worry, though, your hard work has earned you something. Take a little break. Put your essay away for a couple of days, and don't even look at it. When you pick it back up to revise it, you'll be looking at it with a fresh pair of eyes. It sounds kind of funny, but it's true. When you're working on writing your essay and you're in it up to your elbows, it can be difficult to see some of the mistakes that you're making. So, it's important to take a little time to rejuvenate yourself, and then come back to your writing and fix it up, so that it's the best that it can be.

PACE YOURSELF

Say the word *garbage* 25 times. Notice how it starts to sound like it's not really a word. Say it again (just once) in a few minutes, and it'll sound real again. This is sort of what happens when you're working on your essay.

REVISING

Revising, unlike editing, which we'll talk about a bit later, is content based. When revising, you go back over what you've written to make it clearer, more concise, or more organized. The process of revising is simple. Just ask yourself some questions, and while you do that, read over what you have and make sure you're able to answer each question with a definitive *yes*. Here are some questions to ask yourself as you revise.

- Does your introduction draw the reader in?
- Does your introduction have a thesis statement?
- Have you addressed the topic?
- Is your writing clear?
- Have you removed anything that is unnecessary?
- Is your style consistent?
- Is there a good flow from beginning to end?
- Does each paragraph have a topic sentence and supporting ideas?
- Does the conclusion flow logically out of the paragraph that came before it?
- Does your conclusion remind the reader of your thesis and supporting ideas without repeating word for word what you said in your introduction?

INSIDE TRACK

Are all of these questions overwhelming? Focus on one at a time.

EDITING

Editing involves a much closer reading of your writing than revising does. When you edit your paper, you're going to look for errors in grammar, spelling, punctuation, and word usage. To do this, you're going to need to read each sentence very carefully.

Computer versus Paper

Should you edit right on the computer, or should you print out your essay and edit on paper? This is a good question. Each way has its advantages. Your computer's document software probably has a spell-check feature, which is very useful. Definitely take advantage of that feature and always spell-check your work, but for all other editing purposes, printing it out is the best way to go. For one thing, your computer is not as smart as you are and doesn't catch misused words such as *to*, *too*, and *two*. It recognizes all three as real words, so it won't know if you've used them incorrectly. Another reason paper is handy is that you can write on it. So, you can go through and circle things, cross things out, write in the margin, or whatever helps you.

CAUTION!

Steer clear of your computer's grammar check. The computer doesn't know what you intended to say. Only you know that.

What to Look For

As you're reading each sentence of your printed paper carefully, look for the following things:

- consistent tense
- grammar errors
- spelling errors
- punctuation errors

- misused words
- use of active voice wherever possible and avoidance of passive voice
- words and phrases that are repeated too often

NSIDE TRACK

Try using a different color of pen or pencil for each type of error.

Mark It Up!

As you're reading through your essay, mark it up! If you see a word that's used incorrectly, circle it. If you see something that doesn't need to be there, cross it out. But don't stop to fix anything. Just find what's wrong and identify it. If you notice that some of the tenses you used are inconsistent, circle the words or make a note in the margin. It's much easier to tackle one problem at a time once you've identified what the problems are. So once you've finished going through and marking up your paper, read through again and focus on one problem at a time. If you noticed some tense inconsistencies, go back to make sure all the tenses are consistent. If you noticed a particular grammar error popping up now and then, focus on that next and fix all those errors. Just take it one problem at a time.

FUEL FOR THOUGHT

Professional editors have a standard set of symbols that they use in editing. For instance, ¶ means *new paragraph.*

PRACTICE LAP

Read the following essay and then answer the questions.

We have all seen stories on the news and in the newspapers about all the car accidents that have occured downtown in recent months. Some of these accidents have even taken the lives of both car occupants and pedestrians. Although sometimes we feel helpless in the face of these tragic event's, there are actions that our government can take to decrease the amount and the severity of such occurrences. By installing traffic lights at key intersections, lowering the speed limit, and increasing driver's awareness, the number of car accidents can be decreased.

One way to decrease the number of automobile accidents downtown is to install traffic lights at intersections that currantly have only stop signs. Stop signs serve there purpose at intersections with relatively clear traffic patterns, but when the patterns become more complicated, driver's are unsure whom has the right of way on the road. Traffic lights would better organize those intersections, making it much easier for drivers to determine who has the right of way. Driving can be difficult for people who are just learning the rules of the road. Also, some drivers tend to drive straight through stop signs, only slowing down enough for people to think that they have stopped and making crossing the street extremely dangerous for pedestrians, as they may get struck by a car which they thought had stopped.

Pedestrians would also find it safer to cross the street if the speed limit were lower. More accidents occur when cars are flying by at high speeds, because it causes both drivers and pedestrians to have a much shorter time to react to oncoming accidents. Cars themselves, when moving at higher speeds, require a much longer distance in order to stop. This means that the faster a car is going, the more likely it is to rear-end the car in front of it, if that car has to make an unexpected stop. So the number of time a driver has to stop and the number of time that both drivers and pedestrians would have to react is both increased by decreasing the speed limit in the area.

Not only do drivers need time to react but they also need to be aware of what is going on when their behind the wheel. Accidents would also decreese if drivers were more aware while driving. To help drivers become more aware, there are two steps that can be taken. We can add road signs to decrease any confusion regarding the traffic pattern in the area and we can ban cellphone use while driving. A driver who is distracted is much more likely to have an accident then one who is paying attention cell phones are an enormous distraction to a driver.

Cutting down on distractions and increasing the number of road signs will help driver's be more aware while they are behind the wheel. Increased driver awareness, along with a lower speed limit and more traffic lights, will decrease the number of accidents that occur in the downtown area. It is important for our government to take these necessary actions to insure that no more lives are lost in car accidents that can be prevented.

1. Read through the essay and circle all the spelling errors.
2. Put a box around all the grammatical errors.
3. Underline any misused words.
4. Which sentence is out of place?
5. Which sentence is written in the passive voice?
6. Rewrite that sentence in the active voice.
7. What is the thesis statement?

Check your answers on page 101.

LET'S RECAP

If you remember one thing from this chapter, it's that revising and editing are *very* important. No matter how good you think your essay is the moment you stop writing, it can always be improved. Everyone makes mistakes, and most of them are simple and easily fixed. So, always leave time to revise and edit your essay.

The first step in revising is to take a break. Doesn't seem like a step, does it? But it is. Put the essay away and don't look at it for a couple of days. When you come back to it, you'll be able to read it with a new perspective. You're sure to see things you didn't notice as you were writing. Then, as you begin to revise, ask yourself a series of questions and make sure that the content of your essay is as good as it can be. Check your essay for all its necessary parts, and check to make sure all those parts flow together well. Once you've done that, read your essay again and, this time, mark it wherever you see errors in grammar, spelling, word usage, punctuation, and so on.

When you've finished revising and editing, you'll be confident that the essay you turn in is as good as it can be. And that will be a fabulous feeling.

ANSWERS

1. to 3.

We have all seen stories on the news and in the newspapers about all the car accidents that have (occured) downtown in recent months. Some of these accidents have even taken the lives of both car occupants and pedestrians. Although sometimes we feel helpless in the face of these tragic [event's], there are actions that our government can take to decrease the amount and the severity of such occurrences. By installing traffic lights at key intersections, lowering the speed limit, and increasing [driver's] awareness, the number of car accidents can be decreased.

- The word *occured* should be spelled *occurred*.
- *Event's* is not meant to be possessive, so it should not have an apostrophe.
- *Amount* is used only in cases in which you can't actually count the items to which you are referring. *Number* should be used here.

- *Driver's* means belonging to one driver, but the intention of the sentence is to say that the awareness belongs to multiple drivers. The apostrophe should go after the *s*, not before.

One way to decrease the number of automobile accidents downtown is to install traffic lights at intersections that (currantly) have only stop signs. Stop signs serve there purpose at intersections with relatively clear traffic patterns, but when the patterns become more complicated, [driver's] are unsure whom has the right of way on the road. Traffic lights would better organize those intersections, making it much easier for drivers to determine who has the right of way. Driving can be difficult for people who are just learning the rules of the road. Also, some drivers tend to drive straight through stop signs, only slowing down enough for people to think that they have stopped and making crossing the street extremely dangerous for pedestrians, as they may get struck by a car which they thought had stopped.

- The word *currantly* should be spelled *currently*.
- *There* is the wrong word in the context of the sentence. The purpose belongs to the stop signs, so the possessive *their* should be used.
- *Driver's* is meant to be plural, not possessive, in this sentence and, therefore, should not have an apostrophe.
- *Who* should be used here instead of *whom*. *Whom* is used only as a replacement for him, her, or them, none of which makes sense in the sentence. You wouldn't say, *Him has the right of way*. You would say, *He has the right of way*.
- *Which* should be used only to introduce a nonrestrictive clause. *They thought had stopped* is not a nonrestrictive clause. It is an essential part of the sentence, not an aside. You should use *that*.

Pedestrians would also find it safer to cross the street if the speed limit were lower. More accidents occur when cars are flying by at high speeds, because it causes both drivers and pedestrians to have a much shorter time to react to oncoming accidents. Cars themselves, when moving at higher speeds, require a much longer distance in order to stop. This means that the faster a car is going, the more likely it is to rear-end the car in front of it, if that car has to make an unexpected stop. So the number of time a driver has to stop and the number of time that both drivers and pedestrians would have to react [is] both increased by decreasing the speed limit in the area.

- This time, *amount* should be used instead of *number*. Time can be considered only as an amount, unless you are referring to specific measures of time that can be counted, like minutes or hours.
- *Is* should be replaced by *are*, because the subject *drivers and pedestrians* is plural.

[Not only do drivers need time to react but they also need to be aware of what is going on when their behind the wheel.] Accidents would also (decreese) if drivers were more aware while driving. To help drivers become more aware, there are two steps that can be taken. We can add road signs to decrease any confusion regarding the traffic pattern in the area and we can ban cell-phone use while driving. [A driver who is distracted is much more likely to have an accident then one who is paying attention cell phones are an enormous distraction to a driver.]

- The first sentence of this paragraph needs a comma before the *but*, because the first part of the sentence is an introductory clause.
- Also, in that sentence, *their* should be *they're*, the contraction for *they are*.
- *Decreese* is spelled incorrectly; it should be spelled *decrease*.
- The last sentence in the paragraph is a run-on sentence. It is actually two sentences and should be separated by placing either a period or a semicolon after the word *attention*.
- Also, in that sentence, *then* is incorrect. *Than* should be used because a comparison is being made.

Cutting down on distractions and the increasing number of road signs will help [driver's] be more aware while they are behind the wheel. Increased driver awareness, along with a lower speed limit and more traffic lights, will decrease the number of accidents that occur in the downtown area. It is important for our government to take these necessary actions to insure that no more lives are lost in car accidents that can be prevented.

- *Driver's* is possessive but should be plural. The sentence is referring to multiple drivers, so there should not be an apostrophe.
- *Insure* means to secure something from harm. Based on the meaning of the sentence, the correct word to use would be *ensure*, which means to make certain.

4. Driving can be difficult for people who are just learning the rules of the road.
   Although this sentence is sort of related to the rest of the essay in the sense that it is about driving, it's not exactly relevant to the topic. The essay contains no other reference to new drivers.
5. To help drivers become more aware, there are two steps that can be taken.
   The steps is the subject of the sentence, and they are receiving the action of being *taken*.
6. To help drivers become more aware, we can take two steps.
   Now the subject of the sentence is *we*, and we are the ones performing the action. We are the ones who can take the steps to help drivers become more aware. Changing the voice to active fixes the misplaced modifier in the original sentence. *Who* was doing the helping in that sentence? Now the reader knows it was *we*.
7. By installing traffic lights at key intersections, lowering the speed limit, and increasing drivers' awareness, the number of car accidents can be decreased.
   The thesis statement is the last sentence of the introduction and clearly states the main point of the essay.

9 Writing Prompts

WHAT IS A WRITING PROMPT?

A **writing prompt** is basically a set of instructions. If someone said to you, "Write an essay," it would be a bit overwhelming. What are you supposed to write about? It could be anything. Maybe you could write about how elephants communicate with one another, or about what you did on your last birthday, or about how you think your school should have more art classes. All of these topics could make interesting essays, but chances are, the person who wants to read your essay already has an idea of what your essay should be about. A writing prompt directs you to write a specific type of essay about a specific topic.

FUEL FOR THOUGHT

The word *prompt* means "to move to action."

TYPES OF PROMPTS

There are three different types of prompts: *expository*, *narrative*, and *persuasive*. It's helpful to understand each of these, so that when you see them, they will already be familiar to you. Here's a little explanation of each one, with an example so that you get the idea.

Expository

An **expository prompt** directs you to *explain* or *describe* something. It could be anything from explaining how to plan a party to describing the best way to get all your homework completed on time. The key words to look for are *explain* and *describe*. They will clue you in to the fact that you're reading an expository prompt. Here's what one may look like.

> *Advances in technology often have significant impacts on our lives. Explain how a new technological innovation has influenced your life.*

FUEL FOR THOUGHT

The word *expository* comes from the word *exposition*, which means an explanation of something.

Narrative

A **narrative prompt** directs you to *tell a story*. Maybe it will ask you to describe a time when you were scared or what you would do if you didn't go to school one day. Narrative prompts often use the word *time*, so that's a key word for which to watch out. Also, *event* is another key word, because you may be asked to tell the story of a particular event. Here's an example of a narrative prompt.

Sometimes it is said that "Sticks and stones can break your bones, but words can never hurt you," yet words often do hurt us. Describe a time when you were hurt by words.

Persuasive

A **persuasive prompt** directs you to *persuade* someone of something. You may be asked to persuade the reader, but you may also be asked to persuade a hypothetical someone, who won't necessarily read your essay. For instance, you may be asked to persuade the mayor of your town of your opinion regarding a proposal for year-round school. This could be a made-up proposal and even a made-up mayor, but it gives you a topic and direction for your essay. So, a persuasive prompt asks you to persuade someone of your opinion about something. The key words are *persuade* or *convince*. Here's an example of what a persuasive prompt may say.

A friend of yours has asked you if you think he should get a job. Think about whether or not you think it would be a good idea, and write to your friend to persuade him of your opinion.

PACE YOURSELF

Try creating your own prompts. What topics do you think would be interesting to write about? Save them in a folder or envelope for future practice essays.

HOW TO ANSWER A WRITING PROMPT

Step 1: What Kind of Prompt Is It?

The first thing you want to do when answering a writing prompt is to determine which of the three types of prompts it is. This will help you instantly, because you'll know if your essay should be explaining something, telling a story, or persuading someone to agree with something. Let's use the following prompt as an example.

> *Imagine that you've been asked to design a park in your neighborhood. Think about what you would include in your park. How would the space be laid out? How will people in the neighborhood use the park? What kinds of plants would you use? Explain what your park design would look like.*

You know that this is an expository prompt because you are being asked to *explain* something.

Step 2: What's the Topic?

Once you have identified the type of prompt with which you are dealing, your next step is to figure out what the prompt is asking you to write about. In other words, what is the topic? You've already determined that our sample prompt is an expository prompt. So, you will be explaining or describing something in your essay. But what will you be explaining or describing?

> *Imagine that you've been asked to design a park in your neighborhood. Think about what you would include in your park. How would the space be laid out? How will people in the neighborhood use the park? What kinds of plants would you use? Explain what your park design would look like.*

The underlined portions of the prompt show you the topic. You are being asked to *explain what your park design will look like*. Your topic is a *design for your neighborhood park*.

Step 3: What about the Topic?

Now that you know what the topic is, you need to make sure you know what you are supposed to be writing about that topic. It's not enough to know that your topic is *a design for your neighborhood park*. Reading the prompt carefully will tell you exactly what you should be writing about the topic that's been introduced.

> *Imagine that you've been asked to design a park in your neighborhood. Think about what you would include in your park. How would the space be laid out? How will people in the neighborhood use the park? What kinds of plants would you use? Explain what your park design would look like.*

The prompt has given you questions to think about before you start writing. The answers to these questions are what you are going to say about the topic. You're going to be explaining your park design idea, so you will need to include a description of not only what the park will look like physically, but also how it will be utilized by your neighbors.

INSIDE TRACK

Whenever you can, mark up the prompt. Circle sentences or phrases that stand out. Underline sections that seem important.

Step 4: Write!

You know the topic, and you know what you're going to write about that topic, so now you're all set to write. Just go through the steps outlined in this book. Start by doing some prewriting, webbing, and organizing, and then outline and start writing your essay. If you have a time limit in which to write your essay, you may need to cut these steps short, but we'll talk about that in the next chapter. When you're done writing, don't forget to make sure you have a thesis statement as well as well-constructed paragraphs with topic sentences.

Step 5: Have You Answered the Prompt?

The last thing to do is to make sure you've addressed everything that is laid out for you in the prompt. So, reread the prompt one last time, just to check.

PRACTICE LAP

For each of the following prompts, identify what type of prompt it is.

1. Think of a time when you hadn't seen someone in a while and then you saw him or her again. Describe what happened when you reunited.

2. Your friend has decided that he or she wants to start eating a healthier breakfast. Think about what you think he or she should eat. Write to your friend to persuade him or her of your opinion regarding what to eat for a healthy breakfast.

3. Sometimes it is fun to be outdoors. Think about a time when you had a good time outdoors. Describe what you were doing and what made it fun.

4. We all have memories. Think about a memory that you have. Describe that memory and what makes it stand out in your mind.

5. We can all think of songs we enjoy listening to. Think about a song you enjoy and explain why you enjoy listening to that song.

6. Your school principal has decided to ban cell-phone use on school grounds. Do you agree or disagree with this decision? Think about how the ban would affect you and your classmates. Write a letter to your principal persuading him or her of your position regarding the cell-phone ban.

7. You have been told that you need to do three chores at home. Think about which three chores you would choose to do and explain why you would choose those three.

For each of the following prompts, identify both the topic of the prompt and what you are being asked to say about that topic.

8. Sometimes it is fun to redecorate a room in your home. Think about which room in your home you would redecorate. Explain why you would redecorate that room and describe what it would look like when you are finished.

9. Your town council is trying to decide whether to make wireless Internet available for free within the town limits. Do you think this would be a good idea? How would it affect citizens of your town? Write a letter to the town council persuading them of your position on the free wireless Internet.

10. You have a friend who is being teased at school. Give your friend some advice, explaining what he or she should do about the teasing.

11. Your class has decided to grow a vegetable garden outside on the school grounds. What would you grow in the garden, and why? Write down what you will say to your class to persuade them to grow your choice of vegetables.

12. Your town has decided to turn the professional fire department into a volunteer fire department. How do you feel about this decision? How will it affect the citizens of your town? Write a letter to the editor of your local paper to persuade readers of your position regarding the decision to have an all-volunteer fire department.

13. It is said that exercise is a good way to stay in shape. There are many exercises that a person can do. What exercises would you pick to do to stay in shape? Explain why you would choose those exercises.

14. There are many different types of art. Think of a piece of art that you have liked. Explain why you liked that piece of art.

15. Your softball team has decided to get a gift for your coach at the end of the season. What do you think would be a good gift? Write a letter to your teammates persuading them of your opinion regarding the gift for your coach.

LET'S RECAP

Some of your writing assignments may come in the form of a writing prompt. A writing prompt is a set of instructions for your essay. From it, you'll learn the topic on which you are being asked to write and what, specifically, you should be writing about that topic.

There are three kinds of writing prompts, each instructing you to write a slightly different kind of essay. First is the expository prompt. Expository prompts ask you to explain something. The key word here is *explain*. Second is the narrative prompt. Narrative prompts ask you to tell a story. The key words to look for in a narrative prompt are *time* or *event*. Third is the persuasive prompt. Persuasive prompts ask you to persuade someone of something. The key words here are *persuade* or *convince*.

To answer a writing prompt, all you need to do is determine what it is you're being asked to write. Identify which kind of prompt you're dealing with, and then look for key words and any other phrases or questions embedded within the prompt that stand out to you. Locate the topic and what you are being asked to write about that topic. Then, write! When you're done, read through the prompt one last time, just to make sure that you've addressed all aspects of the topic.

ANSWERS

1. narrative
   You are being asked to describe a *time* when you were reunited with someone, which means you will be telling a story.
2. persuasive
   You are being asked to *persuade* your friend.

3. narrative
   You are being asked to describe a *time* when you had fun outdoors. You will tell a story about that time.
4. expository
   You are being asked to *describe* a memory.
5. expository
   You are being asked to *explain* why you enjoy a song.
6. persuasive
   You are being asked to *persuade* your principal of your position regarding the cell-phone ban.
7. expository
   You are being asked to *explain* which chores you would choose and why.
8. Topic = redecorating a room
   What you should write about = which room and what would it look like
9. Topic = free wireless Internet in town
   What you should write about = your position on the issue
10. Topic = a friend being teased
    What you should write about = your advice for your friend
11. Topic = vegetable garden
    What you should write about = what you should grow and why
12. Topic = all-volunteer fire department
    What you should write about = your position on the issue
13. Topic = exercise
    What you should write about = which exercises you would do and why
14. Topic = art
    What you should write about = a piece you've liked and why
15. Topic = gift for coach
    What you should write about = what it should be and why

Timed and Untimed Essay Writing Strategies

Some essays may be assigned far enough in advance that you will have plenty of time to write a fabulous essay. Other essays may be due in only a matter of hours, and you'll wonder how you could possibly write it in such a short period of time. Well, this chapter will take you step by step through the pace of writing each kind of essay. Whether you have three months or just three hours, all you need is a plan of action.

UNTIMED ESSAYS

If asked whether we'd rather have to write a timed essay or an untimed essay, most of us would probably say we'd choose an untimed essay, so that we could, essentially, have as much time as we needed to write it. With so much time, however, you may often find it difficult to avoid procrastinating. Calling an essay *untimed* is a bit misleading. Even *untimed* essays have to be completed at some point; you have some set amount of time to complete your essay. You have a large enough chunk of time that you're not worried about being able to finish it, but how do you budget your time so that you don't end up rushed at the end?

Step 1: Make a Plan

What you need is a long-term plan. The more time you have to spend working on your essay, the better your essay will be. You have more time to think through your ideas, more time to write, and more time to fix any mistakes you may have made along the way. Having more time won't help you, though, if, for instance, you don't budget enough time to revise. This is where the long-term plan comes in.

First, you'll need to establish how much time you have to complete your essay. It could be a week or a month. Whoever assigns you the essay will tell you when it is due. For example, let's pretend you have a month. Once you know that you have a month before your essay is due, you can make yourself a schedule so that your time will be budgeted to include all the necessary steps in creating a great essay.

PACE YOURSELF

Create a short-term schedule for yourself. What is your plan for the next 24 hours?

Creating a Schedule

Let's continue with our pretend time frame of one month. Given one month, you could break down your time this way.

SUN	MON	TUE	WED	THU	FRI	SAT
WEEK 1 Prewrite and outline	→	→	→	→	→	→
WEEK 2 Write	→	→	→	→	→	→
WEEK 3 Write	→	→	→	→	→	→
WEEK 4 Revise and edit	→	→	→	→	→	→

If you choose to make this schedule with one month to write your essay, great! Stick to it! But this is just an example. Let's say you know that you usually take longer to complete the revising and editing stage—give yourself a little bit more time for that. The important thing is to make a schedule and to stick with it. We all have tendencies toward procrastination, but having a schedule really helps you visualize what you need to be doing, and when. If you know that procrastination is a real problem for you and are worried that you may leave all your prewriting to the last day of Week 1, then make yourself an even more detailed schedule. Allot yourself specific amounts of time for free-writing, webbing, and outlining. That way, you'll have smaller, more manageable goals along the way to keep you on track.

Step 2: Brainstorm

If you are not assigned a specific topic for your essay, use this time to brainstorm some topic ideas. Make lists of potential topics and test a few by doing some prewriting to see if the topic would yield enough material for a whole essay. Some topics may seem like great ideas, but when you actually start trying to think of a thesis as well as support for that thesis, you may find that you don't have enough to say about it.

PACE YOURSELF

Talk to people about what you're thinking of writing in your essay. You never know what a conversation may inspire.

Step 3: Start to Organize

Once you have a juicy topic, it's time to begin organizing your thoughts. Use all the methods and tips that we talked about in Chapter 2. Take all your thoughts and ideas and sort them into a web or chart. Sometimes, it can be difficult to understand the importance of organizing even before you make an outline, but imagine making an outline without having determined your main points and how you will support those points. Each step along the way makes the next step in the process easier. So, don't skip this step, even if you're tempted.

At this point in the process, do some research if your essay requires it. This is the time to gather all of the information that will end up in your outline.

Step 4: Make an Outline

Now, make an outline with all the thoughts, ideas, and information that you've gathered. Just as the webbing and charting makes creating the outline easier, making an outline makes writing your paper easier. Having an outline will ensure that your essay is as clear and organized as it can be. Your reader won't wonder what you're talking about halfway through your essay. The outline keeps you on track with your ideas in the same way that making a schedule keeps you on track during the process of writing your paper.

Step 5: Write

You should spend the bulk of your allotted time actually writing your essay. But, because you have purposely scheduled in time to revise and edit when you're finished writing, don't worry about it being perfect. Sometimes it can slow down the flow of writing if you stop to try to rewrite what you just wrote. Concentrate on getting all of your ideas down in sentence and paragraph form, making sure to include all the parts of an essay. You'll be able to go back later and fix your mistakes. Just make sure you stick to your schedule.

Step 6: Revise and Edit

This is one of the most important steps in the essay writing process, because no matter what you've written up to this point, now's your chance to improve it. At this point, you should have a complete essay in front of you. Use this time to read over what you've written as many times as you need to in order to correct any mistakes you may have made along the way. Ask yourself the following questions before you consider yourself absolutely done.

- Does your essay have a compelling introduction that draws the reader in?
- Does your introduction have a clear thesis statement?
- Does each paragraph in your essay have a topic sentence that relates back to the thesis statement in some way?
- Does your essay have a conclusion that restates your thesis without being repetitive?
- Does your writing flow logically and smoothly from one idea to the next?
- Have you eliminated all grammatical errors and errors involving spelling and word usage?
- Have you addressed the assigned topic and/or answered the question?

Step 7: Turn It In

You're done! Congratulations! You should be proud of all the hard work you've put in and of turning in a paper that was written to the best of your ability. Just remember to put your name on it.

PRACTICE LAP

1. Rearrange the following steps of writing an untimed essay into the correct order.
   Revise and Edit
   Make an Outline
   Write
   Start to Organize
   Turn It In
   Make a Plan
   Brainstorm

2. Which of the following is NOT a good question to ask yourself when you're revising?
   a. Does my essay have good flow?
   b. Will I get a good grade?
   c. Do I have an introduction?
   d. Do I have a clear thesis statement?
   e. Are there spelling errors?

Assume you have one month to complete your essay and identify whether the following long-term schedules would be considered a good plan or a bad plan.

3. Week 1: Prewrite
   Week 2: Prewrite
   Week 3: Write
   Week 4: Write

4. Days 1 to 5: Prewrite
   Days 5 to 20: Write
   Days 20 to the due date: Revise

5. Days 1 to 5: Prewrite
   Days 5 to the due date: Write

6. Half of Week 1: Prewrite
   Rest of Week 1, Weeks 2 & 3: Write
   Week 4: Revise

7. Week 1: Write
   Week 2: Write
   Week 3: Write
   Week 4: Revise

Check your answers on page 127.

TIMED ESSAYS

In the previous section, we talked about writing a so-called *untimed* essay, for which you may be given a deceptively long period of time in which to complete your assignment. Now, let's talk about *timed* essays. Timed essays can be quite nerve-wracking. You sit down, you're given a topic, and you have to be done with your essay in, say, three hours. That doesn't seem like enough time! Well, no. It's not enough time to do all the prewriting and webbing and outlining and revising that we've been discussing, but it is enough time to write a quality essay. There are just two things to remember.

Keep it *organized*.
Keep it *simple*.

Okay, now you're sitting down with your assignment in front of you, and you can feel the seconds ticking away. You're already running out of time! Don't panic. Take a deep breath and focus on one step at a time.

Step 1: Come Prepared

The first step in writing a timed essay is to be prepared. Make sure that you eat a good breakfast the morning of the essay and that you get a good amount of sleep the night before. You wouldn't want to be tired and hungry while you're trying to write your essay. Also, make sure to bring with you everything that you may need—a pencil or a pen and some scratch paper if it's allowed. A watch may also come in handy during the essay. That way, you won't have to worry whether or not there is a clock in the room.

INSIDE TRACK

Gather all your supplies together the night before your essay so that you won't be rushed in the morning.

Step 2: Don't Panic

This is an important step. Make sure to relax. Take slow deep breaths. Try not to concentrate on the limited amount of time you have in which to write your essay. If you stay organized and keep it simple, you'll have plenty of time.

FUEL FOR THOUGHT

You'll be so focused on writing your essay that once you start, you'll be finished in a flash.

Step 3: Understand the Topic

Before you can write your essay, you'll need to understand what you are being asked to write. You could work really hard on your essay in the amount of time that you have, but if you don't answer the question or address the topic, then it will all have been a waste. So, take a few minutes to read the assignment carefully, circling any key words or phrases that may help you decide what to include in your essay.

Step 4: Budget Your Time

Just like when you're writing an untimed essay, you need to budget your time when writing a timed essay, so be sure to set aside some time at the beginning to organize your thoughts and some time at the end to revise. However, don't take so long budgeting your time that it eats into your work time. You could even do this step before you sit down to write your essay. If you know in advance how much time you will have, you could make yourself a time budget before you arrive.

Take a minute to think about how much time you have in which to write your essay, and then quickly divide that time into three sections.

Organizing
Writing
Revising

If, for example, you have three hours, you may want to divide your time this way.

half hour = organizing
two hours = writing
half hour = revising

Again, just make sure that you leave time for yourself to revise at the end. It'll feel a lot better to have that time to review your essay, instead of having to write your conclusion in a rush just as someone is saying, "Time's up." If you want to, jot down your time budget somewhere as a reminder.

PACE YOURSELF

Before your essay, practice timing yourself. Get out a practice prompt, give yourself a certain amount of time, and then start. When you're done, think about how you budgeted your time and how you could be more efficient in the future.

Step 5: Short Prewrite and Organize

Don't spend a lot of time on this step, but spend enough to come up with a thesis statement and organize your thoughts. You may want to make a quick web of some sort or just write down your thesis statement and list your supporting ideas. Even though you don't have a lot of time to spare, taking some time to organize your ideas will strengthen your final product and may actually save you time in the long run.

Step 6: Write

Once you have a plan of action, start writing. Remember all the things we've talked about: an introduction with a good thesis statement, clear supporting ideas, strong paragraphs, each with a topic sentence, and a conclusion that reminds the reader of your thesis. Keep these things in mind as you write.

Because you don't have a lot of time, you're not going to be able to write as much as you would for an untimed essay. So, you'll need to be clear and concise. All the same essay writing rules still apply, with regard to needing a thesis statement and strong paragraphs, but you won't have time to go into a great deal of detail. The easiest thing to do is to keep your essay to a basic five-paragraph structure, as follows.

Paragraph 1 = Introduction
Paragraph 2 = Body with Support 1
Paragraph 3 = Body with Support 2
Paragraph 4 = Body with Support 3
Paragraph 5 = Conclusion

If you try to write more, you'll end up with a lot of writing that's not as clear and strong as it would be if you limited the amount you wrote and focused on the quality of your ideas and support. Just remember, it's *quality* that's important, not *quantity*.

CAUTION!

Don't wander off track with your essay. There may be an interesting tangent you'd like to explore, but you have only a short amount of time, so keep your points focused.

PACE YOURSELF

Find a writing prompt and give yourself 30 minutes to write an introduction to your answer. Then, try a different prompt and see if you can write an introduction in 20 minutes.

Step 7: Revise

It's important to leave time at the end to read over your essay and fix any errors that you may have made. You won't have a lot of time, so just perform some abridged revising and editing techniques. As you read through your essay, ask yourself some questions.

- Does my writing flow logically and smoothly from one idea to the next?
- Do any words or phrases stand out as being overused or unneeded?
- Have I included all the important parts of an essay?

And finally, a very important question.

- Have I addressed the assigned topic and/or answered the question?

Then, read through your essay carefully one last time and fix any errors that you may have made in spelling, punctuation, word usage, or grammar.

Step 8: Relax

Time's up. You're done! Sit back, relax, and be proud that you've done your best in the limited amount of time you had. Oh yeah, and make sure you put your name on it.

PRACTICE LAP

8. Which of the following would NOT be a good way to prepare for your timed essay?
  a. eat a good breakfast
  b. read this book
  c. bring a pencil or pen
  d. wear a watch
  e. stay up late

9. Make a time budget for a two-and-a-half-hour essay.

10. Give yourself 20 minutes and plan what you would write for the following essay topic.

> Think of a person who is a good leader. What makes that person a good leader? Explain what qualities a person needs in order to be a good leader.

Check your answers on page 128.

LET'S RECAP

Untimed essays are not exactly untimed. You don't have forever to complete them; they're actually due at some point. But you'll probably have a good amount of time, and we all know what sometimes happens when we have a long time to complete something: We procrastinate. To combat procrastination, make a schedule and stick to it. As soon as you're assigned your essay, make a schedule. Plan out how much time you'll spend prewriting, how much time you'll spend writing, and how much time you'll spend revising and editing. Before you do anything else, make a plan.

Make sure that your plan includes all the necessary steps in the essay writing process. Don't skip prewriting. Don't skip revising. Both are essential if you want to end up with the best possible essay, one that's clear, organized, and error-free. Once you have your plan, start brainstorming, prewriting, and outlining. From that, you will form the basis of your paper. When you're finished writing, revise and edit! This is crucial. If you haven't planned on time for revision, you'll be forced to turn in an essay that could have many mistakes. Wouldn't you feel proud turning in an essay that you knew was the best it could be? Of course you would. So make a plan, stick to it, and don't forget to revise!

Although untimed essays may tempt us into procrastinating, a timed essay can be a lot of pressure. But, if you come prepared and know how you will budget your time, you'll be off to a good start.

Writing a timed essay is similar to writing any other kind of essay. Your actual essay will need all the same parts: an introduction, a body, and a conclusion. Keep it simple, though, because your time is limited. Write a one-paragraph introduction (with a clear thesis statement, of course), a three-paragraph body (one paragraph for each supporting idea), and a one-paragraph conclusion. Don't try to make your essay any more complicated than that.

Before you even get to your timed essay, make sure that you get a good night's sleep, eat a good breakfast, and gather all the supplies you may need. When you're given your assignment, take a few deep breaths. Don't panic. Just go step by step and you'll finish in time. Take a minute or two to understand what you're being asked, and then take another minute or two to budget your time. Make sure to take some time at the beginning to organize your thoughts and take some time at the end to revise. You don't want to be starting your conclusion when your time is up. Just remember to keep it simple and organized. Once you're finished writing, go back over what you've written and correct any errors you may have made. Then, when your time is up, you're done!

If you go into your timed essay well prepared, you'll find it much easier to stay calm and focused. And your essay will reflect that in the end.

ANSWERS

1. Make a Plan
   Brainstorm
   Start to Organize
   Make an Outline
   Write
   Revise and Edit
   Turn It In

2. **b.** If you worry too much about what grade you will receive, you'll lose your focus. Just concentrate on doing the best you can by following all the steps outlined in this book.
3. bad plan
   This plan leaves absolutely no time for revision. Revising and editing your essay is crucial, because it gives you a chance to go back and correct any errors you've made along the way. And as perfect as you try to make your essay, you're bound to make mistakes. It's okay to make mistakes, as long as you build in time to fix them.
4. good plan
   This plan doesn't allow a lot of time for prewriting, but that's okay. You may feel that you don't need that much time. As long as you do the prewriting and leave yourself plenty of time at the end for revision, you'll have a good plan.
5. bad plan
   Like the first plan, this one leaves no time for revision.
6. good plan
   This plan breaks up the month a little bit differently, but still leaves time at the beginning to prewrite, time at the end to revise, and a good chunk of time in the middle to write.
7. bad plan
   This plan has no prewriting scheduled. Without prewriting, you'll find it extremely difficult to start writing. What is your thesis? What are your supporting ideas? What will you say about those ideas? If you don't prewrite and organize your thoughts, you'll have to make it all up as you go along, and you'll most likely end up with an unclear and unorganized essay.
8. **e.** It would not be a good idea to stay up late the night before your timed essay. You may end up being tired while you're trying to write. Or, even if you don't really feel tired, your brain will not be up to its maximum thinking abilities.
9. 20 minutes = Organize
   1 hour 50 minutes = Write
   20 minutes = Revise
   This is a good time budget for a two-and-a-half-hour essay. It starts off with 20 minutes to organize your thoughts, which is plenty of time but

not too long. It includes ample writing time and leaves you 20 minutes at the end to revise. The 20 minutes for revising is key. You'll have time to fix any mistakes and not be rushed at the end.

10. Thesis = To be a good leader, a person should be charismatic, intelligent, and funny.

Support =

1. charismatic to attract followers
2. intelligent so people believe what he or she says
3. funny to entertain so people will be captivated

This is just an example of what your thesis statement and support may look like and one way that you may jot it down. The thesis statement is strong, explaining the necessary characteristics for a good leader. Support for the thesis is an explanation for each characteristic. Why would it be good for a leader to have that characteristic? Of course, if you were to write this essay, you would want to think of more reasons that each characteristic is important and maybe even give some examples of its importance.

Posttest

Just like the pretest, the posttest contains 53 questions. It contains the same types of questions, and it should take you no longer than two hours to complete. After taking the posttest and checking your answers against the answer key that follows, you will see how much you have learned from the lessons in this book. For the questions that you answer incorrectly, read the answer explanations and refer back to the chapter that discusses that particular topic. Good luck!

In the following sentences, circle the word(s) that makes the sentence correct.

1. George and his (friends/friend's) love to (eat/eats) pizza.
2. It seems like everybody likes (their/his) pizza crust thin, but George and his friends like (their/his) pizza crust thick.
3. I can't believe how late (it's/its) gotten.
4. Dan has (less/fewer) soup than I have.
5. (Pineapples/Pineapple's) are a tasty addition to fruit salad.
6. (She/Her) and (me/I) both wear glasses.

7. Both of my (shoes'/shoes) laces are tied in knots.

Identify each of the following sentences as either correct or incorrect.

8. Taxes are due soon I had better get started.
9. Because she cared so much about the plight of the homeless, Harriet decides to volunteer at a homeless shelter on the weekends.
10. My friend was over, so my mother asked him and me if we wanted a snack.
11. The computer, which is old, has completely stopped working.
12. Because of the gusty winds, the bench tipped over.
13. I slipped on the wet grass playing soccer.
14. It's so slippery on the road that one of the car's wheels has lost its grip.

Rewrite the following sentences to make them correct.

15. The United State's flag is red white and blue.
16. Her and I ran a race after school, that ended early today.
17. Everyone in the apartment building has their own mailbox in the lobby.
18. Chad received a present in the mail its his birthday on Friday.
19. He and his brother goes to the movies on the weekends.
20. They went to the movies and buy popcorn.

For each of the following sentences, choose the correct word to fill in the blank.

21. Recently, the temperatures in the area have ____________ widely, making it difficult to decide what to wear.
- **a.** vacated
- **b.** fluctuated
- **c.** rebuilded
- **d.** obstructed
- **e.** misplaced

22. The fact that Mom was mad was ____________ in the way that she was standing with her arms folded.
- **a.** implicit
- **b.** maligned
- **c.** lacerated
- **d.** indolent
- **e.** indistinct

23. We didn't think the play was anything special and, in fact, found it to be quite ____________.
- **a.** ineffable
- **b.** efficient
- **c.** cogent
- **d.** mediocre
- **e.** amenable

24. The cat found itself to be in a bit of a ____________ when it got its tail stuck in the fence.
- **a.** depression
- **b.** redemption
- **c.** rectitude
- **d.** predicament
- **e.** tirade

25. Firefighters came to clear out the area so that nobody would inhale the ________________ fumes that were coming from the burning building.

a. tipsy
b. theoretical
c. unwieldy
d. unique
e. noxious

26. The professor told Casey not to write down what the professor had just said because it was a ________________ piece of information.

a. tireless
b. frivolous
c. vegetative
d. wittingly
e. winsome

27. The burst pipe in the basement created quite a ________________.

a. zephyr
b. treatise
c. deluge
d. superlative
e. solstice

28. Oil spilling into the river may ________________ the water supply of the town.

a. separate
b. retrieve
c. contaminate
d. propel
e. juggle

29. In order to discover more about how the machine would work if it were manufactured, the engineer created a ______________.

a. junction
b. kiln
c. grotto
d. fathom
e. prototype

30. The little girl was full of so much ______________ that she was jumping up and down.

a. vivacity
b. facility
c. extremity
d. dexterity
e. cupidity

31. Yesterday, there was such a sudden ______________ of hail that cars were dented and people had to run for cover.

a. curtsy
b. onslaught
c. boycott
d. adjunct
e. digress

32. The knight rescued the princess from the tower, proving that he was ______________.

a. dilatory
b. itinerant
c. radical
d. gallant
e. stagy

33. After the player caught the ball by the edge of the woods, she had trouble ________________ herself from the bushes.

a. tantalizing
b. extricating
c. satirizing
d. originating
e. henpecking

34. The flowers he gave her were ________________ and were spilling over the edge of the vase.

a. heedless
b. exotic
c. demented
d. audacious
e. bountiful

35. Because the coin collector wanted only ________________ coins, he refused to buy fake ones.

a. choral
b. authentic
c. delectable
d. flamboyant
e. flexible

36. It was difficult to get the bookcase into the house because it was so large and ________________.

a. unwieldy
b. globular
c. ghastly
d. exigent
e. cursory

Identify the topic and focus of the following topic sentences. Circle the topic and put a box around the focus.

37. Learning to swim is not difficult if you follow some simple steps.

38. There are many reasons why watching dog shows on television is enjoyable.

39. Every household should have a smoke detector for a number of reasons.

40. There are a number of ways you can make macaroni and cheese.

41. By following some simple steps, a person can increase his or her vocabulary.

Write a topic sentence using each topic and focus listed.

42. Topic = starting a lemonade stand
Focus = steps to create a lemonade stand

43. Topic = developing your own photographs
Focus = steps in the process

44. Topic = seeing an eye doctor
Focus = reasons it's beneficial

45. Topic = being a good student
Focus = factors that contribute

46. Topic = revising and editing
Focus = ways they strengthen your essay

Choose the correct answer to the following multiple-choice questions.

47. The topic sentence of a deductive paragraph is ____________.
- **a.** optional
- **b.** at the end
- **c.** more important than a thesis
- **d.** at the beginning
- **e.** none of the above

48. Using only inductive paragraphs can make your writing seem ___________.
- **a.** exciting
- **b.** intelligent
- **c.** dull
- **d.** naïve
- **e.** creative

Read the following paragraph and then answer the questions that follow.

> A person must prepare in many ways to be able to run a marathon successfully. Marathons are 26.2-mile running races that take place all over the world. Recently, there was a marathon in New York. Marathons are so difficult to complete that a person must be physically, mentally, and emotionally prepared. A marathon runner must physically prepare by running almost every day for months in advance. Each run should get longer and longer to prepare the body for the 26.2-mile run. Visualizations are used to prepare mentally. For example, a runner may visualize him- or herself crossing the finish line without trouble. For emotional support, a runner may surround him- or herself with other runners who are having similar experiences or people who support his or her goal of completing the race.

49. What is the topic sentence of the paragraph?

50. What kind of paragraph is this?

a. inductive
b. deductive

51. Which sentence in the paragraph is out of place and should be omitted?

Write an essay for each of the following writing prompts.

52. Many careers involve serving the community in some way. Think of a career that involves serving the community. Would you like to have that career? Explain why you would or would not enjoy that career.

53. Sometimes the weather can alter our plans for the day. Think of a time when you had to change your plans because of the weather. What was your original plan? What kind of weather event occurred? What was your new plan? Describe how the weather altered your plans for the day.

ANSWERS

1. friends . . . eat
The word *friends* in the sentence is plural, not possessive, so there should be no apostrophe before the *s*. One person *eats* pizza, but many people *eat* pizza. *George and his friends* is plural, so the verb must also be in the plural form.

2. his . . . their
Everybody refers to every one person and is singular, so the pronoun should also be singular (*his* or *her*). *George and his friends* is plural, so the pronoun *their* should be plural as well.

3. it's
In this sentence, *it's* is being used as a contraction for *it has*, so an apostrophe is needed.

4. less
Because you can't count individual amounts of soup (unless you are comparing measured amounts, like tablespoons), *less* should be used in this comparison.

5. Pineapples

Pineapple just needs an *s* to be plural. An *'s* would make the word possessive.

6. she . . . I

She wears glasses and *I wear glasses*, so *She and I wear glasses*.

7. shoes'

The laces belong to the shoes, and *shoes* is plural, so an apostrophe is needed after the *s* in *shoes*.

8. incorrect

This sentence contains two independent clauses that need to be separated by either a period or a semicolon. You may write the sentence like this: *Taxes are due soon; I had better get started.*

9. incorrect

The comma in this sentence is correctly separating an introductory clause. The error is in the verb tenses. If she *cared* in the past, then she must also *decide* in the past. *Decides* should be *decided*.

10. correct

My friend was over is correctly separated by a comma, because it needs to be separated from the second half of the sentence, which is also an independent clause. *Him and me* is correct, because *my mother asked him* and *my mother asked me*, so she asked *him and me*.

11. correct

Which is old is a nonrestrictive clause and is correctly set apart from the rest of the sentence with commas.

12. correct

Because of the gusty winds is an introductory clause and is correctly set off from the rest of the sentence with a comma.

13. incorrect

The sentence has a misplaced modifier, which makes it seem as if the grass were playing soccer. To clear up the confusion, you would need to rearrange the sentence to read, *While playing soccer, I slipped on the wet grass.*

14. correct
Both *its* and *it's* are used correctly in this sentence. *It's* is being used as a contraction for *it is*, and *its* is being used to show that *it* (the wheel) possesses the grip. *Car's wheels* is also correct, because the multiple wheels belong to a single car.

15. The United States' flag is red, white, and blue.
The *United States* is already plural, so, to make a possessive, you just need to add an apostrophe after the s. Also, this sentence should have commas separating the list of colors.

16. She and I ran a race after school, which ended early today.
You wouldn't say, *Her ran the race*. You would say, *She ran the race*, so the correct pronouns in this case are *She* and *I*. The end of the sentence is a nonrestrictive clause and is correctly set apart with a comma, but the word *which*, not *that*, should be used in nonrestrictive clauses.

17. Everyone in the apartment building has her own mailbox in the lobby.
Everyone is the same as every one person, so the correct pronoun to use is *her* (or *his*). *Her* is singular, and *their* is plural. The noun and the pronoun in the sentence should agree.

18. Chad received a present in the mail; it's his birthday on Friday.
This sentence is actually two independent clauses that need to be separated by correct punctuation. Placing a semicolon after the word *mail* fixes the error. Also, *its* should be *it's* in this case, because it is being used as a contraction for *it is*.

19. He and his brother go to the movies on the weekends.
He and his brother is plural, so the verb needs to be in plural form. Two people *go* to the movies, while only one person *goes* to the movies.

20. They went to the movies and bought popcorn.
Both verbs in the sentence need to be the same tense. If they *went* to the movies in the past, then they *bought* popcorn in the past as well.

21. **b.** This is a cause-and-effect sentence completion question. What could the temperatures have been like recently to cause difficult clothing decisions? *Fluctuating* means unpredictable or irregular.

22. **a.** This is a restatement sentence completion question. The correct word is already somehow defined for us in the sentence. We can tell that Mom is mad by the way her arms are folded, so the meaning of the missing word should have to do with something unspoken and understood. *Implicit* means unspoken or understood.

23. **d.** This is another restatement question. We know that the play wasn't anything special, so the missing word should mean something similar. *Mediocre* means average or ordinary.

24. **d.** This is a comparison sentence completion question. An example of the missing word's meaning appears in the sentence. A cat getting its tail stuck in a fence is in a what? *Predicament* means a dilemma or a mess.

25. **e.** This is a cause-and-effect sentence completion question. What kind of fumes would cause firefighters to clear the area? *Noxious* means toxic or harmful.

26. **b.** This is a cause-and-effect sentence completion question. What type of information could the professor have given Casey that would not need to be written down? *Frivolous* means trivial.

27. **c.** This is a cause-and-effect sentence completion question. What would be the effect of a pipe bursting? A *deluge* is a flood.

28. **c.** This is a cause-and-effect sentence completion question. What would the effect of an oil spill be on water supply of the town? *Contaminate* means pollute or infect.

29. **e.** This is a restatement sentence completion question. The missing word is defined in the sentence. What would the engineer create with the purpose of seeing how it works before it was manufactured? A *prototype* is an example or a trial.

30. **a.** This is a cause-and-effect sentence completion question. What would make the girl jump up and down? *Vivacity* means liveliness or energy.

31. **b.** This is a restatement sentence completion question. The missing word is defined in the sentence. Which choice means a sudden appearance of something dangerous that sends people running for cover? An *onslaught* is an attack or ambush.

32. **d.** This is a comparison sentence completion question. The missing word is a characteristic of the knight. We know that the knight rescued the princess, so which word would describe a knight willing to do that? *Gallant* means heroic or brave.

33. **b.** This is a contrast sentence completion question. We gather from the sentence that the ballplayer has fallen into the bushes. What would be the opposite of falling into the bushes? To *extricate* means to remove or disentangle.

34. **e.** This is a restatement sentence completion question. The missing word is already defined for us, so which word would mean something like spilling over the edge? *Bountiful* means abundant or plentiful.

35. **b.** This is a contrast sentence completion question. We know that the coin collector doesn't want fake coins; he wants the opposite of fake. *Authentic* means real or genuine.

36. **a.** This is a cause-and-effect sentence completion question. What characteristic of the bookcase would make it difficult to get into the house? *Unwieldy* means awkward or bulky.

37. TOPIC FOCUS
(Learning to swim) is not difficult if you follow some [simple steps].

38. FOCUS TOPIC
There are many [reasons] why (watching dog shows on television) is
FOCUS
[enjoyable].

39. FOCUS TOPIC FOCUS
[Every household should have] a (smoke detector) for a number of [reasons].

40. FOCUS TOPIC
There are a number of [ways] you can (make macaroni and cheese).

41. FOCUS TOPIC
By following some [simple steps], a person can (increase his or her vocabulary).

The given answers to the following questions are only examples of topic sentences that you could write based on the information given. Just make sure that your sentence includes both the topic and the focus.

42. *Creating a lemonade stand is easy if you follow some simple steps.*

43. *By following some steps in a simple process, a person can develop his or her own photographs.*

44. *Making regular visits to an eye doctor can be beneficial to your health.*

45. *There are a few factors that contribute to a person being a good student.*

46. *Revising and editing your essay will strengthen it in many ways.*

47. **d.** In a deductive paragraph, the topic sentence appears at the beginning.

48. **c.** Inductive paragraphs, when used consistently, can make your writing seem dull. Similar to the passive voice, inductive paragraphs are an indirect way of writing. Keep your writing direct by using deductive paragraphs and the active voice.

49. *A person must prepare in many ways to be able to run a marathon successfully.*

This sentence introduces what the paragraph will be about (the topic) and what about that topic will be discussed in the rest of the paragraph (the focus).

50. **b.** This is a deductive paragraph, because the topic sentence is the first sentence of the paragraph.

51. *Recently, there was a marathon in New York.*

This sentence, while related to marathons in general and related specifically to the sentence that comes before it in the paragraph, doesn't exactly fit in with what is being discussed. The fact that there was a marathon recently in New York has little or nothing to do with how a marathon runner may prepare to run the race.

52. *When thinking of careers that serve the community in some way, most people probably think of firefighting and police service. Both firefighters and police officers serve the community in a direct way by protecting its citizens. Other careers, however, are more indirect in how they serve the community. One of those careers is teaching. Of all the careers that serve the community in which I live, teaching is the one that I would enjoy most. The facts that it serves the community, offers a good work schedule, and provides the opportunity to work with children all make teaching a terrific career.*

The opportunity to work with children appeals to me for a couple of reasons. One reason is that I think I would enjoy helping children reach their goals. Many children start out in school wanting to become a certain kind of person in the world. Some may want to be scientists and others may want to be sculptors, but whatever their aspirations may be, school is where they learn the tools that will enable them to achieve their goals. And teachers give them those tools. The other reason is that working with children allows for a less formal work environment. The school day itself is always changing as students learn various academic subjects. I'd much rather be in a school than in an office, where I would probably sit at a desk in front of a computer all day.

Teachers not only have the flexibility to avoid sitting at a desk all day, but also have an ideal work schedule. Unlike most professionals, teachers have the entire summer off. I would love to be able to use my summers for activities other than work. Specifically, I could use the time off from work to explore my hobbies, travel around the country, and spend valuable time with my family, all of which are important to me. Teachers also have a day-to-day schedule that differs from other professions. In most districts, school is over fairly early in the day, so I could also use that time to accomplish some everyday tasks, like running errands and cooking dinner.

The ability to run errands in the afternoon after school is only a small perk compared to the pleasure of knowing that you are serving your community. There are always opportunities to give back, but to be able to support yourself with a career that you know is making a difference in other people's lives is a tremendous advantage. I have had some pretty amazing teachers who have supported me in my interest and passion for learning certain subjects. To be able to give back by becoming a teacher myself seems like an ideal career.

Becoming a teacher, like the ones who have made a difference in my life, would give me frequent opportunities to contribute to my community. I would enjoy working with children and helping them along their journey to become whatever they want to become in their lives, as well as the perfect work schedule that comes with the job. Although teaching is not the career that comes immediately to mind when we think of serving the community in which we live, I believe that it is equally as important as being a firefighter or a police officer and is certainly the career I would choose to make a difference in the lives of others.

The preceding essay is just an example of what your answer to the writing prompt may look like. Of course, your essay will be different. Just make sure that your essay has an introduction with a clear thesis statement; plenty of supporting paragraphs, each with a topic sentence; and a conclusion that wraps everything up without being repetitive. It should also be free of any grammatical, spelling, or word usage errors.

53. *Meteorologists do their best to predict the weather, but they don't always get it right. Sometimes, the weather surprises even them by changing in what seems like an instant. Of course, even when meteorologists do predict the weather correctly, we don't always pay attention, so we sometimes find ourselves in a situation in which the weather literally rains on our parade. I can think of one time in particular when the weather altered my plans.*

It was a sunny, warm weekend afternoon in late spring, and my mother and I were on a mission. I had been assigned a project in my science class and had to collect as many different wildflower species as I could find and then accurately identify them. My mother was helping me, and we decided that the perfect place to look for wildflowers was the state park, which was about a half-hour drive from our house. We set out for the park after lunch, excited about our flower search. It had been a warm morning, but by the time we got to the park, it had really heated up. Water bottles and flower-collecting supplies in hand, we parked the car and started walking down one of the many paths that wandered its way through the woods.

As we walked down the path, we noticed the sky beginning to darken, but we hadn't heard anything about rain, so we walked on. About 20 minutes (and a few flower species) later, we heard a rumble. One rumble turned into two, and we realized it was thunder. Standing in the middle of the woods was definitely not the place we wanted to be in a thunderstorm, so we turned around to go back to the car. At just that moment, we saw a flash, heard an enormous clap, and felt a few fat drops of rain landing on our arms. It was clear that our flower hunt was over. We ran as fast as we could back to the car in the steadily increasing downpour.

The rain continued during our drive home until we were about five minutes away from the house. Stopped at a red light, just as we were feeling like our wildflower search had been a major bust because of the storm, we spotted a large clump of flowers on the side of the road. We pulled over and got out to find three different types of flowers that we hadn't seen at the park. They were beautiful, an excellent addition to my science project. Back in the car, we finished the drive home, feeling like we had completed our mission after all.

The storm had put a major dent in our plans. We were all set to spend the day at the state park, wandering the paths and collecting wildflowers for my science project, when a large, unexpected thunderstorm materialized. Our plans had to change. We couldn't stay out in the woods during a storm and would have had to make plans to return to the park a different day. Fortunately for us, on the way home, we found some interesting flowers by the side of the road. So, although Mother Nature didn't accommodate our plan for that day, I was still able to complete my science project.

This essay is also just an example of what you could write to answer the prompt in question 53. Because it is a narrative prompt, your essay will be a little bit different from the way it would be normally. You're being asked to tell a story instead of making some sort of argument, so you won't have a traditional thesis statement. But you should have a statement that introduces the story you will be telling. You should also make sure in a narrative essay that you address all the aspects of the story that you're asked in the prompt to tell. This prompt asked you to describe a time that a weather event changed your plans for the day. Make sure you touch on what your plans were, what happened with the weather, and how it altered your plans. It also needs to be a well-told tale that's free of grammatical, spelling, and word usage errors.

Glossary

Active voice: A way of writing in which the subject of a sentence performs the action of the sentence.

Body: The middle, and longest, part of your essay, in which you defend or support the thesis you set forth in your introduction.

Brainstorm: The process of thinking of ideas by writing down in a list the first things that come to mind.

Cause and effect: A type of sentence completion question in which the correct answer choice is either the cause or the effect of something already defined in the sentence.

Clue phrase: A word or words in a sentence completion question that hint at what type of question it is.

Comma splice: Two complete sentences incorrectly joined by a comma.

Comparison: A type of sentence completion question in which the correct answer choice is compared to something already defined in the sentence.

Complete sentence: A sentence that contains both a subject and a predicate and expresses a complete thought.

Conclusion: The last paragraph of your essay, in which you restate your thesis.

Contrast: A type of sentence completion question in which the correct answer choice is contrasted with something already defined in the sentence.

Deductive paragraph: A type of paragraph in which the topic sentence is the first sentence.

Dependent clause: A group of words that contains a subject and a verb but cannot stand alone and does not express a complete thought.

Editing: The process of reading over your paper and making changes in grammar, spelling, punctuation, and word usage.

Expository: A type of prompt that asks you to explain something.

Flow chart: An organizational chart that starts at the top of the page and flows downward to create a visual representation of your ideas.

Focus: In a topic sentence, this is what is being said about the topic.

Free-write: A form of brainstorming in which you write any ideas about the topic that come to you, without editing yourself.

Fresh eyes: The new perspective on your essay that you obtain from putting it away for a while and then coming back to it.

Grammar: The rules of language.

Helping verb: A verb that is paired with another verb to give the reader a better sense of when the action took place.

Independent clause: A set of words that includes a subject and a verb and expresses a complete thought.

Inductive paragraph: A type of paragraph in which the topic sentence is the last sentence.

Introduction: The first paragraph of your essay, in which you introduce the reader to your thesis.

Introductory clause: A dependent clause that introduces the main part of the sentence.

Irregular verb: A verb that changes form in the past tense.

Long-term plan: A plan devised to prevent procrastination while writing an untimed essay.

Misplaced modifier: A phrase that appears in the wrong place in a sentence, making it unclear who or what is performing the action of the sentence.

Narrative prompt: A type of writing prompt that asks you to tell a story.

Nonrestrictive clause: A group of words that is not essential to the meaning of the rest of the sentence.

Organize: To arrange your ideas into the order in which they will appear in your essay.

Outline: A written chart that helps you organize and order your ideas.

Passive voice: A way of writing in which the subject of the sentence does not directly perform the action of the sentence.

Past participle: A verb form in the past tense that relies on a helping verb.

Persuasive: A type of writing prompt that asks you to change someone's mind.

Predicate: The verb (or action) of the sentence; a necessary component of a complete sentence.

Prewrite: To brainstorm and organize ideas before you start to write your essay.

Pronoun: A word such as *he* or *her* that is used to replace a noun in a sentence.

Restatement: A type of sentence completion question in which the correct answer choice is already defined in the sentence.

Revision: The process of reading over your paper and making changes to its content.

Run-on sentence: Two or more sentences joined without punctuation.

Sentence completion question: A question that asks you to choose the correct word to complete a sentence.

Sentence fragment: A group of words that lacks either a subject or a predicate; a phrase.

Subject: What (or whom) a sentence is about; a necessary component in a complete sentence.

Subject/verb agreement: The rule that the subject and verb of a sentence must either both be plural or both be singular.

Tense shift: An instance in which verbs in the same sentence are in different tenses.

Thesis statement: A sentence in which you state your main argument or point.

Timed essay: An assigned paper that must be written in one sitting, in a limited time frame.

Topic: The subject of your paragraph; one of the two parts of a topic sentence.

Topic sentence: A statement in your paragraph, containing a topic and a focus, that tells the reader what the paragraph is about.

Untimed essay: An assigned paper that you have a relatively long time to write.

Web: A visual representation of your ideas with the main idea at the center and supporting ideas branching out from that center.

Writing prompt: An assignment or set of instructions for an essay.